Retirement
on a
Shoestring

Retirement on a Shoestring

John Howells

Gateway Books

Printed in the United States of America

Gateway Books

San Rafael, CA

Distributed by Publishers Group West

**Library of Congress Catalog Card Number
92-52700**

10 9 8 7 6 5 4 3 2

Other Gateway books by John Howells:

Choose Mexico (1985. 1988), by John Howells and Donald
Merwin
How to retire on $400 a month in comfortable, safe and pic-
turesque surroundings. This book has sold over 140,000 copies.

Choose Latin America (1986), by John Howells
Leisurely travel experiences and retirement throughout the marvelous world of Mexico, Costa Rica, Brazil, Uruguay, Argentina, Chile and other Latin countries of the western hemisphere.
(Out-of-print, but available at many libraries.)

RV Travel in Mexico (1989), by John Howells
A handbook for the RV traveler who is ready to enter the exciting adventures of mobile living in Mexico. A guide to smooth
traveling, finding the safest places to stay, and how to truly
enjoy the unique experiences that Mexico has to offer. Lists
hundreds of RV parks throughout the country.

Choose Spain (1990), by John Howells and Bettie Magee
How to enjoy Spain and Portugal through leisurely travel or
retirement. A complete guide to the Iberian Peninsula for those
who want a different way of travel.

Where to Retire (1991), by John Howells
A comprehensive guide to America's best retirement places.
Detailed information on hundreds of choice retirement sites,
with both statistical data and personal observations on what
makes them attractive.

Contents

Introduction

Retirement on a Shoestring

While doing research on a previous book on retirement, my wife and I drove coast-to-coast twice, zig-zagging back and forth in search of desirable places to retire. We traveled many thousands of miles by car, motorhome and airline. As we visited cities, towns and hamlets, we tried to imagine ourselves actually living in each place. We looked at rentals, property for sale and checked prices in stores and restaurants. We examined the newspaper classified sections for prevailing wages and mobile homes for sale. In each location, we estimated how much income the average retired couple would need to live there. Early on, we discovered that the cost of living varies markedly from region to region.

One day, as we were having lunch in a small mining town in Idaho, we began wondering what we could do on a *minimum* budget. What if our worst fears were realized; our only income a Social Security check? (According to the Social Security Administration, the average benefit for couples is about $960 monthly; for single males, $670 and even less for single females.) Although an income of this magnitude would barely cover rent in many towns we've researched, hundreds of thousands have to get by on a Social Security check; that's their only source of income. We began to wonder: suppose we were to choose to retire here; how would we make out in this town?

We checked a real estate office for their cheapest listings and found an older, two-bedroom frame house in town selling for $10,000 and another outside of town, a two-bedroom brick for $15,000. Don't misunderstand, we're not suggesting that you can go just anywhere and pick up a house for $10,000! These houses were priced like this because the mines had closed, there were no jobs, and businesses were struggling. Houses were very difficult

11

to peddle because everyone wanted to sell and nobody wanted to buy. Empty houses weren't renting because the tenants were moving away to find jobs. As retirees, however, low employment opportunities wouldn't matter nearly as much as low housing costs.

We located the first house—a narrow, two-story Victorian, about a five-minute walk from the nearest grocery store—and peeked through the windows. As you can imagine, it needed paint and cleaning, it was small—just a living room and dining room downstairs and two bedrooms above—yet it looked sturdy. Except for its double-wide lot, this house looked identical to "picturesque" old houses in our home town of Pacific Grove, California, places that commonly sell for more than $200,000. Suppose we were to rent a place like this? The local newspaper listed several homes for $175 a month, some furnished.

We figured out a tentative "bare bones" budget for living modestly but comfortably in this town and we came up with a figure of $820. The table below shows how we arrived at this figure. Automobile expense accounted for $110. While car expense might seem like a big chunk out of the budget, living here without a car would be difficult. (This is true of most small towns without local or national bus service.) Of course, this budget doesn't allow for items like automobile depreciation, life insurance premiums, club dues or loan payments or other expenses that vary with individual circumstances. Assuming that we could qualify for Medicare, and given the fact that our car is paid for and that we've already cashed in our life insurance, we added $60 for supplementary medical insurance. This brings us to $820 a month. Yes, we *could* make all of our basic expenses on Social Security! That amount wouldn't cover rent and utilities in some other towns we've visited!

Rent, small 2-bdr	$175
Food	$225
Utilities (summer only)	$60
Cable TV	$20
Automobile gas & maint.	$55
Automobile insurance	$55
Clothing and laundry	$50
Medicare supplement	$60
Property taxes	$20
Miscellaneous	$110
Total	**$820**

Please note that throughout this book the cost of living refers only to basic expenses, those items most people say they cannot avoid. Obviously, individual circumstances differ. To our sample budgets you'll need to add your own extras. If, when you retire, you still have car payments, mortgage payments, medical insurance, back taxes, alimony, gambling debts and numerous bar tabs, you don't need a book on how to retire on a minimum income—you need a book on how to win the lottery. For those of you who have no medical coverage, you don't need someone telling you that you are in trouble. Until our government and medical establishment catches up with the rest of the world in assuring medical care for its citizens, 37 million Americans will be without protection. Hopefully, you are one of those lucky enough to afford the care you need. If not, what can I say? You have plenty of company.

Home Base

At first glance, a small western mining town such as the one we were researching, would appear to be a great place to retire. Set in a picturesque, tree-covered canyon, its small downtown section looks like something out of a western movie set. But, frankly, living year-round in such a place would be out of the question for us. Our biggest objection: the bitterly cold winters in Idaho. We couldn't imagine ourselves stoking a wood fire day and night, trying to keep the house warm through long, sub-zero winters. Another problem is the lack of community services for senior citizens. Towns where population and taxpayers are dwindling have few funds left over for senior citizens. This is an all-important consideration, as we shall see later on in this book.

Even though we recognized that this town was not the perfect retirement setting, we became interested in the possibility of using it as a "home base." The extra lot would make a great place to store our small motorhome while we enjoy an inexpensive summer and fall, living in a peaceful, gorgeous mountain setting. When winter threatens, we could store our things, winter-proof the house and drive our motorhome to Arizona, Florida or Mexico for inexpensive RV living. Small-town safety and neighbors would protect our valuables while we were on the road.

Granted, this small mining town isn't representative of the normal, everyday real estate market. Yet, dedicated bargain hunters can find similar conditions in many parts of the country. A factory goes bankrupt and workers follow jobs elsewhere. Logging and fishing industries fall into doldrums. A military base closes its barracks and destroys the local economy. Any number of work-related disasters can turn a wonderful residential community into a nightmare for workers. Yet, this disaster can be a windfall for those who don't *have* to work. Later in the book, we'll talk about how to locate these bargains.

Mind you, finding depressed towns is just one solution for low-cost retirement. If we all crowded into these places, costs would rise until they would no longer be bargains. Furthermore, too many depressed towns are depressed simply because they are boring places to live! Because you can buy a house for $15,000 does not guarantee you will enjoy living there. If the most exciting thing to do is sit on your front porch rocker and count passing cars, you might as well enter a rest home.

Cost of Living Varies

Again, as we studied retirement lifestyles and economic conditions in various sections of the country, we were impressed by wide differences in the cost of living. Some couples reported they couldn't make it on less than $20,000 a year, while others do okay on incomes of $12,000 a year.

Unfortunately, there are millions of folks in the United States to whom a $12,000 income would be a blessing. Folks who have to take minimum wage jobs find it even tougher, with incomes around $9,000 a year, or less than $175 a week.

This book isn't just for those who need to survive on minimal budgets. Most readers probably look forward to perfectly adequate incomes, but they'd rather not spend it all on basic living expenses. Cutting back on one area of the budget will release funds for some luxury or a treat. Putting money aside for emergencies is a prudent move. Knowing that it's possible to live on a less than average income is a reassuring thought; whether it is necessary or not, you'll always have that "ace in the hole."

Other readers, while they may own property worth a small fortune, don't feel particularly rich. Owning a home doesn't do a thing toward boosting income. Home ownership usually *absorbs* money from the homeowner's monthly income. After paying taxes, maintenance and miscellaneous costs of home ownership, some folks are lucky to have enough left over to buy groceries—even though their home may be worth hundreds of thousands of dollars. Therefore, this book tries to present strategies for maximizing the use of scarce retirement dollars for *everybody*, no matter what their level of income or how high their net worth.

Chapter One

Senior Boomers' Generation

We've heard a lot about the baby boomers' generation, that titanic wave of children born right after the end of World War II and the ensuing decade. It caused a tremendous expansion of home building, school construction and other activities designed to keep up with the growing number of children. An enormous amount of our tax dollars went to raise and educate these baby boomers. They were the ones who used to say, "Don't trust anyone over 30!" Remember? Well, that was 25 years ago, and today, these baby boomers are middle aged and heading for retirement themselves. They are getting bald, with gray hair and sagging bellies. Don't trust anyone over 30, indeed!

Curiously, the baby boom generation opted not to have so many children. The birth rate declined—to one of the lowest points in our history. The number of children has been shrinking while the number of elderly is on the rise.

One reason there are so many more retirees is that we are living longer. In 1900, the average length of a woman's life was 48 years, today it's almost 82 years. Men traditionally die earlier, so their life span is closer to 75 years. Of course, you realize that "life span" averages in all those who die in childhood, adolescence and middle age. It doesn't mean you men will probably die at age 75! When you reach age 75 in good health, you could easily have another 15 years left to your life expectancy. In fact, the fastest growing segment of the population is the group of senior citizens over 85!

Since we are living longer than ever before, and since so many are passing the age of retirement, this country is now undergoing a *Senior Boomer* generation! Demographers estimate that before long, those over 65 years of age will outnumber teenagers by a two-to-one margin. A problem then arises when you consider that although our taxes supported our parents and grandparents when we were working, fewer taxpayers in the younger generation are going to be supporting us! When the baby boomers join today's senior boomers in our Golden Years of retirement, our grandkids are going to have one hell of a time covering their share of Social Security, Medicare and other senior citizen programs. Maybe they'll be saying, "Don't trust anyone over 65!"

Therefore, it just makes good sense to do some planning, to decide how we retirees are going to cope with the future. If we could get the Administration and Congress to cooperate by cutting back on multi-billion dollar boondoggles and trillion dollar military waste, we'd have a chance. According to New York Senator Moynihan, the government is siphoning over $5 billion a year from Social Security income and diverting the money to disguise budget deficits. Oh yes, they're putting paper I.O.U.s into the drawer, planning on paying it back with deflated dollars way down the line. In the meantime, the $5 billion is not being used for the purpose intended.

Of course, all you can do about government neglect is to voice your opinion and vote. Chances are nobody will listen and you will be out-voted (that's always been my experience). So you need to carefully look at all alternatives for retirement—no matter how much income you will have. If you approach the problem positively and sensibly, you'll find that retirement is something to look forward to, rather than dread.

Golden Retirement Years

When people speak of retirement, the phrase "golden years" commonly comes to mind. Golden, because these years are considered to be a reward—a substantial reward for a lifetime of productive work and loyalty to the company. Most workers eagerly look forward to these happy years as the time when they can enjoy the fruits of their labor, to bask in the sunshine of leisure time. A company pension, stock dividends, annuities, interest on savings plus Social Security provides the income to enjoy this new, carefree career as a retiree.

Unfortunately, not everyone has a company pension to cushion their "golden years." Not everyone has had the good fortune to build up an investment portfolio that pays lavish dividends. For all too many, the main source of retirement dollars will be Social Security benefits—which averaged a little over $960 per couple in 1991. When Social Security checks do arrive, they are dismally inadequate. To be fair, we must recognize that Social Security was never designed as a retirement fund, but rather as a *supplement* to retirement.

The worst-case scenarios are those folks who thought they were adequately covered for retirement only to discover that their retirement plans went south when their employers went bankrupt. Others, who invested heavily in savings and loan retirement bonds, find they are holding worthless paper for all their years of thrift. A friend of ours—a minister in a small-town church—invested his savings and much of his meager income into an insurance annuity. Then, just before his planned retirement, the promised $20,000 a year annuity disappeared into the insurance company's bankruptcy proceedings. The company had traded his retirement money for junk bonds. In the decade of the 1990s, pension plan failures and insurance annuity bankruptcies could surpass the 1980s savings and loan scandals.

It isn't just folks on Social Security who need to plan on getting by on a shoestring. Those workers who were forced into early retirement because of automation, corporate mergers or industrial doldrums won't qualify for Social Security until they reach retirement age. Other workers, whose skills or crafts have been eliminated by modern technology, often have no hope of finding new jobs. All of the above are forced to live on savings and income from part-time jobs. Therefore, this book is designed to be of help to those involuntary retirees.

Poverty Line

Do you earn over $6,268 a year as a single person? Then congratulations. According to the U.S. government, you are *not* poor! If you are married, your income must be less than $7,905 to be considered poor. That's about $120 a week for a single person and $152 for a couple. If you earn more than that, these administration policymakers will nonchalantly tell you that you are too affluent to be entitled to many federal programs aimed at helping the country's poor. How they arrive at this figure is difficult to understand. Yet $6,268 a year is what the fat cats figure is an adequate income for an ordinary citizen to live on. That's only $522 a month! I'd be willing to bet that the average congressman spends more than $522 in monthly payments on his imported Mercedes-Benz. Yet, that's what the administration arrogantly considers an adequate living income.

To compound matters, we have government officials complaining that today's retirement generation is *too affluent!* They feel that too much is being spent on the elderly, at the expense of the country's youth. They cut Medicare benefits and threaten Social Security payments at the same time that they increase their own salaries and medical benefits. By the government's own statistics, over three and a half million senior citizens are living below the poverty line. In 1990 alone, an additional 295,000 persons over 65 slipped into poverty. (Figures on 1991 weren't in at the time of writing.) Women over 65 have double the poverty rate of men of the same age; more than 15 percent fall into this category. Because women's wages are traditionally less than men's, women's Social Security payments are also low—disgracefully low.

Despite our complaints that things are going downhill for the elderly, things are not likely to change for the better. In fact, we must face the fact that the trend will continue—at least through the next decade. That is what this book is all about: facing facts and planning to live with them.

Chapter Two

Retirement Strategies

How do folks retire on Social Security or its equivalent? Do not expect a magic formula here. Unless you have been used to living on a limited income over the past years, it's going to take some adjusting. Not only adjusting financially, but mentally as well. The old notion of "keeping up with the Joneses" needs to be set aside. Instead of feeling depressed because the neighbors have a new Buick every other year, you need to feel proud that you don't waste money on frills, and that your old Plymouth takes you just as many places, and perhaps more. Without having to scrape up the payments for a new car, you can have money left over to enjoy life's good things.

One strategy for low-cost retirement is to take control of the two most expensive parts of your budget: housing and utilities. Expenses such as food, clothing, automobile, and so forth don't vary much between locales. Since most goods are sold by large national chains, retail prices are often exactly the same anywhere you go. But housing is largely based on construction labor costs plus supply and demand for rentals and purchases. Labor costs vary widely from place to place. Utility rates also vary from community to community, but the biggest factor is weather, and how much heating or air conditioning is needed.

Housing Costs

Real estate prices and the level of rents have an extremely broad range throughout the country. Houses that sell for $375,000 in Connecticut can be duplicated in Maryland for $195,000 or in Texas for $95,000. Places that rent for $900 a month in one city can have counterparts in equally nice (or nicer) neighborhoods for $250 elsewhere, a potential saving of $650 a month.

We mailed questionnaires to retirees in all parts of the country inquiring about housing and other living costs in their areas. When we averaged the several hundred responses we received, we got figures that differed significantly from those in the Department of Labor's monthly cost-of-living index, probably because the government's figures average in all incomes and expenditures, including families with exceptionally high monthly incomes. Our questionnaires were targeted at low-income, retired folks, people who know how to economize and get along on very little. Their comments were very enlightening.

For example, many reported that two-bedroom apartments in their area rented for $250 a month, but that two-bedroom houses rented for only $150. These figures ran counter to the Chamber of Commerce statistics for a given town in two ways. For one thing, both rents seemed very low, and normally houses rent for more than apartments. We solved this puzzle when we found that in smaller towns, particularly in the Deep South, the major building emphasis in recent years has been on apartments, so landlords asked top rent for them, whereas most homes were older, and harder to rent out, so tenants enjoy lower costs. The second factor is that our questionnaires were filled out by people on tight budgets, who wouldn't be interested in Yuppie-type houses or apartments.

Other Costs

Some homes require $250 a month for winter heat and $175 a month for summer air conditioning, whereas in other parts of the country $30 a month covers heat and nothing is needed for air conditioning. (We'll discuss this in Chapter Five.) Now, any month that you save $650 a month on rent and $220 a month on heating bills—that means $870 extra in your pocket. In some parts of the country, that extra $870 could cover *all* your other living expenses for the month!

Another cost that varies wildly from one part of the country to another is medical care. Of course, doctors and hospitals are expensive anywhere, but some places—notably the larger cities—really have a problem. Let's hope you are covered by good medical insurance; if not, then the cost of getting sick should also fit into your formula for finding an ideal retirement home. Should you have continuing medical problems and little or no insurance, a careful investigation of hospital and office-visit charges is most important.

Move Away From Your Home?

Does that mean that you must move away, to a low-cost area for inexpensive retirement? To another city? To another state? Not always, even though many folks find moving is the best course of action. They realize that their choice of places to live has largely been determined by their jobs. Now that they no longer have to work, they can measure the advantages of living somewhere else with a different yardstick. They are free to live anywhere they please. They can consider living in Florida, Arizona or Oregon, or *anywhere*. However, if you absolutely cannot picture yourselves living elsewhere, there are alternatives you can look into right in your own community.

The first thing to do is scrutinize your present housing situation. You may be surprised to find there are ways to dramatically cut your present housing expenditures and without leaving your home town. Let's examine some common beliefs about housing and see if there aren't some changes which could make a big difference in your lifestyle.

Sacred Home Ownership

Most readers who will be retiring in the 1990s entered adulthood during an era of cheap and abundant real estate. Buying a house was easy. In the years after World War II, up until the '70s, when inflation pushed the real estate prices past the clouds, anyone with a few hundred dollars in savings could buy a home. Monthly payments were less than rent. For the first time in history, home ownership became so common that it was taken for granted. Our generation grew up with the conviction that it made little sense *not* to own a house. I recall that I bought my first home in 1958 for $850 down, including closing costs. The price was $14,000 with payments of around $100 a month. A similar house would rent for about $125 a month, so the deal was irresistible. Home ownership was doubly important during our working years, since the interest and property taxes we paid were deductible, thus reducing our income taxes.

In those days one man's salary could support a family, send the kids to college and maintain a moderate suburban, two-car lifestyle. Most housewives didn't have to work; they stayed home to take care of the house and the kids. A visit to the doctor was $10, and adequate health insurance cost $20 a month. We made the best cars, television sets and sewing machines money could buy and we enjoyed the highest living standard in the entire world. Those were the *good old days* everyone talks about.

You don't need to be reminded that times have changed. Today, we make the best bombers, missiles and tanks, but we buy our autos, sewing machines and TVs from foreign countries. College tuition is so high that both parents and children must borrow heavily to get a quality education. Today, young married couples take it for granted that both will work until retirement. What ever happened to the "Ozzie and Harriet Nelson" scenario of the wife being the homemaker while the husband earns the daily bread? Today, unless their parents can dredge up the down payment, young adults will be renting for the rest of their lives. Even if they manage the down payment, they both will have to work full time in order to make the monthly payments, which today are usually far *higher* than rent on a similar place. Yes, things have changed.

This decline has come gradually, with little fanfare; it's come relatively unnoticed. Many of those of who bought homes in the '50s or '60s take it for granted that property appreciation will continue on and on to infinity. Maybe it will, although the way the market has been behaving the past couple of years leads me to believe that we could be in a long-term slump. The puzzling thing is: who is going to buy these houses once the older generation is ready to begin selling them off? An entire generation could be shut out of the market unless prices drop drastically.

In any event, the retirement-age generation tends to cling to the conviction that owning a home is essential for stability and safety. They would rather cut back on their budget drastically than lose the feeling of permanence and security that home ownership provides. This is fine for those who can afford to live where they are upon retirement, those who have enough income that their lifestyles won't change appreciably when they no longer have weekly paychecks. Still others, even though they may be strapped somewhat, feel that staying in their home is worth it. After all, the grandkids live nearby and all of their neighbors are close friends.

However, you may find it interesting to examine your attitudes toward home ownership, and see if alternatives might be worth exploring.

Costs of Home Ownership

I have a friend who is nearing retirement, and although he will have a small monthly income, he is confident that he will make out okay. "After all, my house is paid for now, and I'll live rent-free," he explains. "I may have to pinch pennies from time to time, that's true, but at least I'll always have a roof over my head."

We talked about his financial situation, which did look somewhat flat. The company he worked for had no pension or retirement plan. He had little in savings, having put most of his extra money into paying off the house. But on paper, he was fairly well off. After all, his house had appreciated in value over the years, as did much of California real estate, and was now worth nearly $250,000. (In other areas of the country, a comparable home could sell for as little as $95,000.)

With the paid-for house plus his stock investments and IRAs, my friend's net worth was over a quarter of a million bucks. Mostly on paper, of course. His total retirement income was going to be around $12,000 a year, or $1,000 a month. Yes, he and his wife could get by—just barely. But my question is: Why on earth should anyone worth a quarter of a million dollars have to pinch pennies and do without luxuries?

When I suggested that he might sell the house, put the money into a safe investment and live off the interest, he was shocked. To him, that sounded totally irresponsible. After all, a paid-for house is a ticket to security, isn't it? "I will live rent free," he reiterated. "I'd have to pay at least a thousand a month to rent a place like this. That's my entire retirement income!"

Try as I might, I could not convince him that he wouldn't be living "rent-free." The fact is, the cost of living in a paid-for home is equal to the income *lost* by not having the home's equity invested in high-grade securities. A business considers its store, office or factory as a capital investment, and your home is exactly the same type of investment. For example, in my friend's case the after-taxes net on his home would be over $200,000 (figuring his one-time, $125,000 exemption). Even in the current fluctuating market, it was possible to find safe investments paying from eight to ten percent—utility stocks or government-guaranteed "Ginnie Maes," for instance. These investments have been traditionally solid and safe. At 8.8% (what GNMAs are currently paying) my friend's house would return almost $1,500 a month in dividends.

Therefore, the actual cost of living in his own home is $1,500 a month ($18,000 a year) plus taxes, insurance and upkeep which adds another $3,000 a year. Suppose he were to sell his home, and then rent a neighboring place for $1,000 a month—allowing the landlord to pay taxes, insurance and repairs—his gross income would be then be $30,000 a year instead of $12,000. Plus, he wouldn't have to fork over $3,000 for real estate taxes, insurance and upkeep. Finally, he would have an additional $200,000 in tangible wealth, quickly available in cash.

This case may seem extreme, since most readers of this book don't have $250,000 homes. Furthermore, in most parts of the country homes haven't experienced this kind of runaway inflation. Therefore, don't think that I am urging everyone to sell their homes when they retire. For many that would be a terrible mistake. In order for this strategy to work there should be a wide difference between local market values and national values. An additional thing to bear in mind is that property ownership is usually a hedge against inflation. Should the economy go into an inflationary spiral, property probably will go up. On the other hand, should we see a continuing weakening of the market, with many houses for sale and few who can afford to buy, they could go the opposite direction. Making a decision to pull down equity is not easy, and it shouldn't be made until all factors are considered and you take a deep look into that old crystal ball.

Why *Not* Rent?

If, after analyzing your situation, you find you would be better off using your home equity as a cash investment, you might consider the implications of owning versus renting a home. One benefit of renting is that the landlord is responsible for repairing that leaky roof and fixing the toilet, not you or your spouse. Another happy thought is the knowledge that you don't *have* to live there. When your lease is up, you are perfectly free to look for a better place. Since you aren't tied to a particular locality, you are free to go someplace where rents are cheaper. For example: an apartment that rents for $225 a month in Daytona Beach, Florida or Austin, Texas couldn't be duplicated in Chicago for less than $650 a month. Strange as it might seem, some folks would actually rather live in Florida than Illinois.

What is the biggest disadvantage in renting? I often hear the reply, "It's like pouring money down a rathole." Maybe there was a time in your life when that was true, when you were earning good wages and when those high property taxes and interest payments brought you a tidy income tax refund at the end of the year. And, during the time when housing was appreciating at a high yearly rate, and when capital gains were taxed at a maximum of 20 percent, you had a point. But today, the situation is different. Since your retirement income will probably be low (and your Social Security nontaxable), you'll have little income to shelter with tax breaks from home ownership. The real estate market has cooled off, with some financial experts predicting an end to the steady appreciation of the past. The so-called tax "reform" laws stripped away some advantages of property ownership, and it's possible that there are even worse laws to come.

No, home ownership isn't necessarily the best retirement strategy! Let's take the case of some friends of ours, a couple who had been paying $720 a month rent for an apartment—a nice place with a swimming pool and an exercise room, plus organized activities in the clubhouse. They decided to buy a home in a new development. The price was $145,000. Because of their age, the lender required $33,000 down. Their payments came to $1,148 a month, including taxes and insurance (for a 20-year loan with a low 8 3/4% interest rate). This meant an extra $428 a month added to their outgoing funds.

"Well, with the taxes and interest on the loan," they told me, "we'll get a tax break. With the apartment rent, we got nothing back at the end of the year. Renting is like pouring money down a rathole." Is it? They had to sell most of their stocks to make the down payment, stocks which paid $230 a month in dividends. If you add the loss of income to the payments, we find that it costs

$1,378 a month to live in a place not much larger than their apartment—$658 *more* every month.

Suddenly, they found that they have to budget carefully to make the payments; they have to forgo some luxuries. They cut down on ski trips, dining out, impulse buying and other extras they'd become accustomed to before they had to pay out that extra $658 a month. Did they benefit? Yes, because of interest and property taxes, they paid no income tax that year. But since their retirement income was minimal and mostly tax-exempt anyway, they saved very little on taxes.

A few years ago, when real estate was continually rising in value, it wouldn't be unreasonable to expect the resale value of the home to increase by five to ten percent in a year, but this just wasn't happening in that particular market. One year later, neighboring homes were still selling at the same price. Yet, even if the home had increased in value, it wasn't money they could spend until they actually sold the place and went back to renting—where they were in the first place. The same principle also applies to the amount of the loan that had been paid down. Until they finally sell, the profit is in their imagination. No matter how you figure it, had they stayed in an apartment, they would have had an extra $7,896 in their pockets to spend that year. Some day, when property begins to appreciate and when they have their loan paid down, perhaps they will sell and make a tidy profit. In the meantime, they are spending their retirement years investing in the future. They do, however, have the security of living in their own home, and for some folks that's very important.

Home ownership, even though the payments are high, clearly makes sense for a young couple whose earning power will probably grow over the years. As time goes by, they pay off the loan with larger paychecks, with dollars that will probably shrink from inflation. They are building for the future, just as you did at their age. But before you enter an expensive, long-term commitment to build for the future, you might want to consider whether it wouldn't be better to invest your money in your *retirement* rather than in some nebulous future 30 years down the line. Will you be able to enjoy your money as much 30 years from now as you can today? How old will you be then? In short, don't automatically fall for the "down the rathole" line. Figure out the financial advantages for yourself realistically, with an eye on today, not the future.

Homes at 1960s Prices

Some people absolutely cannot bear the thought of retiring without owning their own home. A castle that belongs to them alone, even though a small castle, is more than a luxury; it's a necessity. Having to sell the home they've lived in for years would be too much of a hardship, unless they could replace the home with a less-expensive place of similar quality. In most cases, this will require a move to another part of the country—a place where prices haven't kept pace with the galloping inflation of the '70s and '80s.

Finding these places was particularly exciting for us as Californians who live in an area where costs have soared out of reason. Our mind set is such that any house costing less than $200,000 probably has something terribly wrong with its neighborhood, or lacks some amenity, such as wall-to-wall floors. When we traveled through the "Sunbelt" states, places like Louisiana, Georgia or the Carolinas, we were continually astonished to find nice homes selling for as low as $45,000— places which we would find very comfortable.

While traveling about Florida, checking real estate for my book *WHERE TO RETIRE*, we drove past an elegant golf course development, with homes arranged near the tees so residents could play golf practically from their back yard. We weren't going to stop, because these homes seemed so far out of our financial scope that it would obviously be a waste of time. But, just to see how the rich folks live, we paused to take a look.

The homes sat on huge lots, with lovely trees and landscaping. Each house had a built-in, covered lanai, individual bathrooms for each bedroom, plus a common bath off the kitchen. Even the smallest house seemed huge, the design making it seem much larger than its two bedrooms and 1,800 square feet. Should this house be in a similar California location, the price would easily top $500,000. The Florida price? $80,000 with the contractor willing to bargain from there.

However, even though $80,000 seems like a steal to our way of thinking, we realize that even that is out of reach for the majority of retired folks. But in the same part of Florida, we looked at many homes (not on the golf course) which were selling for as little as half of the $80,000 figure. In addition, we were favorably impressed by the great values and convenience in mobile home living. (More about that in Chapter Six.)

Before I leave you with an impression that California is an impossible place to retire on a shoestring, let me assure you that there are places in that state where the cost of living is as inexpensive as just about anywhere you might wish to retire. The "Motherlode" country is a good example. That picturesque and historic area where gold was discovered and mined back in the days of the '49ers is now being discovered by modern-day retirees. Property there is inexpensive, the climate is mild and the Sierra foothill country is great for outdoor recreation. In many areas, a house on a large, wooded parcel can be found for $50,000, whereas a smaller home on a narrow lot in one of California's high-price neighborhoods would cost $250,000. And on the coast, in places like Eureka—where it never freezes and never gets hot—housing prices are as low as we've seen anywhere.

Luxury Apartments at Bargain Prices

An interesting development came out of the wild-west financial rodeo put on by savings-and-loan cowboys in the 1980s. They were responsible for an abundance of luxury apartment complexes throughout popular retirement areas. With S&L money flowing freely, promoters and contractors raced full speed ahead to build apartment complexes before the money ran out. It didn't seem to matter that there were already too many apartments in an area. The idea was to borrow money, build, make a profit and move on to the next project. Let the government worry about cleaning up after them.

The Savings and Loan cowboys claim that their institutions "lost" billions of dollars, as if the dollars were misplaced or lost on the way to the store or something. The truth is, the money isn't lost at all, it's simply been transferred to other people's pockets while apartment complexes and office buildings have been transferred to bankruptcy court. The bad news is that taxpayers will pick up the final bill for all of this, but the good news is that these complexes make wonderfully affordable retirement havens.

Throughout the South, particularly in Florida and Texas, renters have a wide choice of apartments with rents that often start at less than $300 a month. We looked at one complex in Austin, Texas where efficiencies rented for $250 and one-bedrooms at $285 a month. This was one of the larger places, which featured two swimming pools, tennis courts, putting greens, exercise rooms and hiking paths. Because of this competition, older apartment complexes frequently offer one-bedroom apartments for as little as $200 a month.

Near Daytona Beach, Florida, we saw a two-bedroom apartment with air conditioning, two swimming pools, lighted tennis courts and 24-hour emergency service—renting for $450. A one-bedroom place rented for $335. One retired couple explained, "We had looked at a lovely house for $80,000 and almost bought it before deciding to rent an apartment here. That $80,000 in utility stocks brings in $466 a month. Our rent is only $450, so we live rent-free."

Throughout the areas where apartments are in oversupply, you'll find free, full-color booklets and brochures listing the larger apartment complexes complete with color photos of the grounds and facilities. Almost any shopping center will have these booklets, along with real estate catalogs, which also make interesting reading for those interested in buying rather than renting. The places described are fairly new and well-appointed. Older units will of course be much less.

Affordable Houses

Wherever you find S&L money spent on apartments, you'll also find overbuilding of subdivisions and tract developments. An oversupply of houses naturally depresses the asking prices of homes. A good example of this was the Denver area, where a weekly 16-page listing of houses for sale by the government has kept the market depressed for a long time.

Some typical offerings at the end of 1991 were:

1612 sq. ft., 4 bdrm., 2 bath, Duplex, Ranch—$35,000.
783 sq. ft., 2 bdrm., 1 bath, 1 garage Ranch with covered patio and fence—$32,000.
735 sq. ft., 2 bdrm., 1 bath, carport, Ranch—$15,000.
747 sq. ft., 2 bdrm., 1 bath, covered patio, Ranch—$13,500.

It isn't only S&L problems that bring real estate bargains to the surface. Any number of factors coming together at one time can seriously depress the market. A perfect example of this is Bisbee, Arizona. This is a small mining town, with old brick Victorian buildings in a picturesque canyon setting. The town's prosperity came to an abrupt halt when the Phelps-Dodge Corporation decided to close down the mines. Without employment, families began leaving Bisbee, selling their homes when they could, abandoning them when they could not. At one point you could buy a *furnished* home for $4,000 or less. Some changed hands for as little as $500.

Naturally when the news got out, retirees began taking advantage of these bargains. Today, Bisbee is regaining its prosperity because of this influx of retirement money. Ajo, Arizona, also a mining town, underwent the same experience. Almost overnight, 600 houses went on the market! In a town of 3,500 inhabitants, you can imagine what this would do to prices.

These kinds of give-away prices usually don't last forever; they gradually inch upward to a more sane level. But they will occur any time an economy collapses. The future bargains will predictably occur where the government is closing military bases. For those looking for inexpensive housing, keep your eye open for depressed areas.

Prices will be low when one or more industries fall into hard times and suspend operations. An excellent example of this is Aberdeen, Washington. Here is a town that depended upon fishing and lumber for its livelihood. Both occupations paid good money and the area prospered. Then foreign boats, with their 30-mile long dragnets began cleaning out the fish. Japanese factory ships started buying raw logs, processing them with low-paid Filipino workers, then selling finished lumber products to our consumers. The economy fluttered to a standstill. Fishing boats stayed in port. Lumber mills closed down. As people left the area, houses went on the market, but few buyers were interested.

Many towns in Washington and Oregon have been hit hard by the lumber industry's demise and most are suffering economic doldrums to one degree or another. I use Aberdeen simply as an example. In late 1991, we saw houses offered for as little as $15,000. We don't know if they were selling. We talked to a couple who had just moved there from California. They were thrilled with their home purchase. "It sits on three acres, on a hill overlooking the bay and the ocean," the husband said. "It has four bedrooms, each with its own fireplace, and a huge fireplace in the living room. It's a regular mansion, and we only paid $85,000!" In their California neighborhood, that wouldn't have bought a two-car garage.

The following are a few of the real estate bargains listed at the time of our research visi⁺ Three-bedrooms, fenced yard, large workshop and garage area: $29,500, FHA. Two-bedroom home, completely remodeled, new appliances, new roof: $16,500. There was also a duplex listed for $14,500 and many other places listed for under $30,000. To be objective, many of these places probably sound better than they actually look, but were it not for the ailing economy, most would sell for two or three times the price.

Sharing Housing

In Europe, the concept of house sharing is traditional, as it was in the United States in the early part of this century. During the depression, people thought nothing of families doubling up to share expenses as well as living quarters. A large house can easily accommodate many more people than usually live there. After World War II, a tremendous housing boom made housing readily available and cheap. It then became almost obligatory for every family to own its own little piece of real estate. Shared housing and double-family living became a thing of the past.

Today, with real estate priced out of reach for many people, the idea of house sharing is returning to the American scene. For those who are retired and who don't own a home, or for those who can no longer afford the burdens of home ownership, the notion of house sharing is especially attractive. For those who own a large house and who find the expenses of maintaining it burdensome, sharing is one way to cut costs and make money at the same time.

Group living turns out to be a very efficient as well as convenient way to cut living costs. This is particularly true in some of the more desirable but expensive locations. "If we were to rent a home in this neighborhood," said one couple, "we would have to pay at least $1,000 for rent and utilities. That just wasn't in the cards. We found another couple and a single lady to go in with us and we've cut our rent expenses to about $350 a month."

How do you find these situations? The most common contact is the classified section of your daily newspaper. The number of "housemates wanted" advertisements grows in direct proportion to the increases in housing costs. There are also private and non-profit agencies that specialize in placing individuals in shared housing. Your telephone book's classified section will put you in touch with these agencies.

Not that shared housing is just for retirement-age people. Many of these arrangements are multi-generational "families" in which young, middle-aged and elderly live as one cooperative unit. Others are organized according to sex; women often prefer to live with other women rather than have disruptive menfolk dirtying up the house (as we men are entirely capable of doing).

Obviously, in order to make a success of one of these situations, the group's members must be compatible. This isn't the place for someone who is rigid, closed-minded or who doesn't like being around people. Making the decision to try a shared housing lifestyle requires that you not only investigate the situation very thoroughly, but you also must objectively analyze your own personality. Ask yourself some questions. Do noise and confusion disturb you? Would pets bother you? Would you be terribly upset if someone weren't as neat as you are? Or if a living companion left underwear hanging on the shower curtain? If these things bother you, or if you are notorious for the offenses mentioned above, you should think things over carefully before making a decision. In any event, see if you can't do a trial month's stay to make sure everyone is like-minded and compatible.

Other considerations: Will the space be adequate? How much of the house will be yours besides the bedroom? Will you have room for your hobbies? How are decisions made in the house? Is it a democracy or is someone in charge—perhaps the owner or the original tenant? Neither arrangement is preferable to the other, but you ought to know how it works in advance. If the person in charge is strict but fair, everyone knows where the boundaries are and precisely what the responsibilities are, there should be few problems. But if that person is a tyrant, you may be better off elsewhere. On the other hand, a democratic management—with each resident politicking, lobbying and arguing heatedly over each and every excruciating detail of life in the house—can be just as bad. A happy medium is always the best path.

There should be sharing of work responsibilities, chores and perhaps cooking. Often the housemates take turns cooking supper, giving the others a welcome break. "There are ten of us living in our house," said one lady as she detailed her experiences in shared housing. "Each of us is responsible for preparing three dinners every month, and for cleaning up afterward. That means that except for our three chore days, we have dinner waiting for us every night. We can watch the evening news or read a novel and relax, before and after dinner. The dinners are excellent, too, because each of us cooks our favorite meals, and tries to outdo the others!"

Further questions are: Will you be close to shopping and transportation? If you have an auto, will you have a parking space? You also need to decide the kind of house-partners group you'd like to live with. Some groups behave like small, extended families, while others are more formal, with relationships on a neighborly level rather than family. A larger group gives more of an opportunity to choose friends and to spread expenses over a larger base.

Intentional Community Living

Shared housing doesn't always involve casual or informal groups getting together to share a house. There is a growing movement toward planned, or "intentional," communities. Though sometimes these are small, family-type affairs, many are larger groups, more like clubs, where people with common interests band together to forge new lifestyles and to share expenses and experiences. The intentional community differs from ordinary shared housing in that there is usually a common goal or special shared beliefs among the participants. They think of themselves as "members" rather than simply "neighbors." Ecological concerns are a prevalent theme of these intentional communities.

Many of these experiments are outgrowths of communities which started during the "hippie" era; others are more modern in origin. But, let's remember that the hippie era was some 25 years in the past; the youthful 25-year-olds of those days are now passing through middle-age, on the fast track toward senior citizen status! Other communities are religiously oriented, often receiving funds from a church. I found all spectrums of religious beliefs represented in intentional communities, from hard-shell Baptists, to nature conservation, even one community with a spiritual focus which combined "feminist witchcraft and Buddhism!"

Most intentional communities are owned by members, but often will provide free board and room in return for a specified amount of work. Other groups pay a stipend, and others require a sharing of expenses. Some charge a monthly fee plus work requirements in exchange for residence and seminars. There are communities for women only, some for couples, others for mixed and intergenerational members. Residents work at chores such as kitchen and garden pursuits, teaching, housekeeping, maintenance and a variety of other jobs. Some facilities are located on farms, others in forest or desert settings while still others are urban collectives. Recently a friend visited several intentional communities and reported enthusiastically on two, one of which she intends to join upon retirement. The fee is $330 a month plus 20 hours a week of work in exchange for all meals, nice living quarters and an exciting intellectual ambiance. (At her request, I am withholding the name of this community because of her fears that readers might flood the place with applications before her retirement.)

A complete list of these places can be found in the *Intentional Communities Directory* (see appendix). Be aware that many of these communities are in the process of formation, and may never get off the ground, so be cautious about investing time and money in a mere pipe dream. Many do not actively solicit new members, so don't think you can simply drop in and take up residence. First you need to contact the group to see if there are any openings and if your interests coincide.

This last point is most important. Just because an organization offers inexpensive living doesn't mean you will be happy there. One community listing looked fine until I discovered that the residents were divided equally between straight, gay/lesbian, bisexual and undecided sexual propensities. Suppose I don't fit into *any* of the above categories, what then? Another group, still in the process of forming, plans on building an undersea village where you will be surrounded by the "awesome beauty of the sea."

Continuing Care Retirement Communities

As the retiree population grows ever larger, there is a corresponding increment in the number of complexes devoted exclusively to this market. An increasingly popular development in retirement communities is the concept of long-range, total care facilities. There are three conceptual stages of retirement involved in these developments. First: houses, cottages or apartments for those who want to be totally independent and who prefer to cook meals for themselves. Next comes a stage when folks aren't quite up to doing their own cooking (or are fed up with it), or who might have trouble taking care of themselves. These residents live in apartments, but take meals in the dining room. Finally, there is a stage where skilled nursing care and a traditional nursing home environment is provided in hospital-type rooms if and when they become too infirm to take care of themselves.

Some of these complexes are very, very expensive. Obviously, given the exorbitant cost of medical care in this country, you can understand why. Recently we heard of one place that requires a $400,000 investment (non-refundable on death) and $2,000 a month for expenses. However, because of ever increasing competition, there are a few full-service retirement homes that are reasonable. The least expensive place we found charged about $35,000 to enter and about $690 a month for expenses. This was in Coos Bay, Oregon, a place called Evergreen Court. A monthly income of around $1,000 is required, and some financial net worth is also required. This is not exactly "retirement on a shoestring," but if that's the type of security you're looking for, you can find it with some investigation.

One couple, who moved into one of these lifetime care units said, "When we retired and moved to this part of the country, our only question was whether to buy a house or to rent. This is a compromise between the two." They bought into this complex ten years earlier, both at the age of 60. At the time of the interview they were thinking of giving up their villa and moving into the second stage of the complex. "A nice thing about this arrangement is that we keep pace with our friends. The friends we know as golfing or bridge partners will be with us in the next stage. If they aren't ready to move yet, they soon will be. As we grow older and our interests change, we move along together."

Limited-Care Communities

For those who are unwilling or unable to pay the expensive entrance fees of continuing care, there is an alternative more practical for budget retirement: a retirement community *without* extensive health care. These are usually stand-alone facilities, that is to say, without medical care of any kind, although sometimes a nurse is on call. Although each unit—whether an efficiency, one- or two- bedroom apartment—has a full kitchen, meals are usually served in a dining room. These facilities are becoming competitive, and some bargains can be found. The major difference is that you must be able to take care of yourself without medical supervision. Depending upon where it's located, prices for these places can start as low as mid-$600 a month range, including meals, housekeeping services and all utilities except for telephone. This is an ideal arrangement for singles who don't want to bother with full housekeeping. Examples of this type of facility are found in Chapter Nine.

According to Retirement Housing Foundation, more than three million Americans now live this way, an increase of 300 percent over the past 15 years. Furthermore, nearly 250,000 live in continuing-care communities as described above.

A boom in new retirement housing of this type is evident throughout the country, with construction not keeping pace with demand. When you consider recent studies which show that the number of Americans over 85 years of age will top 24 million in the next half century, the problem should be apparent.

For a time, the U.S. government attempted to do something about low-cost housing through Housing and Urban Development (HUD) programs. Government money subsidized both the construction and monthly rentals for qualifying retirees. However, the outlook today is bleak indeed, with continuing cuts in the funding. For example, back in 1976, HUD allocated $750 million to subsidize 25,000 low-cost housing units. Despite a continually growing number of poverty-line retirees, the money was reduced on a continuing basis until in 1990, the allocation was $450 million for less than 5,000 units. Then came the Persian Gulf War, and the allocation was cut by 80 percent, to less than 1,000 units.

According to a recent survey, in 1991 there were 250,000 low-income retirees on waiting lists for low-cost retirement facilities. The odds of being accepted were about 15%. The odds for 1992 will be even lower, for there will be fewer new units to help. Perhaps the next letter you write to your congressman or senator should cover this injustice.

The largest non-profit provider of subsidized retirement facilities—Retirement Housing Foundation—can send you a list of their facilities and information on how to apply. They operate over 110 retirement communities in 24 states (and Puerto Rico). The units are HUD approved, and the tenants' rents are partly subsidized by HUD. In others, rents are not subsidized, which means that residents pay a deposit and competitive rents, although somewhat lower than a conventional commercial facility because of the HUD low-interest mortgages.

Retirement Housing Foundation manages a total of 6,926 subsidized units and 3,752 non-subsidized units. These include independent-living arrangements, assisted-living and skilled-nursing units. Information about Retirement Housing Foundation's facilities can be obtained by writing 401 E. Ocean Blvd., #300, Long Beach, CA 90802.

Chapter Three

Now It's Your Turn!

All your life you've paid federal income tax and most likely, you've paid state income taxes as well. Maybe you've even been nicked for city or county income taxes. If you own property, you don't have to be told that you've paid a wagonload of dollars to city, county and state governments over the years. If you didn't own property, and just rented a house or apartment all your life, don't feel smug and think that you've avoided paying property taxes. Actually, you've graciously included them in your monthly rent payments. The landlord simply paid the money over to the government for you. When his taxes went up, so did your rent.

Now, add the state, county and city sales taxes you've paid over your lifetime, and you begin to get an idea of how much money you've forked over to the government. You'll never know for sure, because every time you buy something from the store, the cost of the manufacturer's taxes are passed along to you as part of the purchase price: corporation taxes, sales taxes, property taxes, import duties, payroll taxes and who knows what else.

You've often wondered what the hell they do with all this money, haven't you? (If you haven't, you must have an exceptionally high threshold of pain.) We often hear politicians taking cheap shots at food stamps, Medicare, Social Security and other programs as being wasteful. If you listen carefully to their solutions, you'll find that we could solve all our budget problems simply by cutting back on programs that help the elderly, the needy and the unfortunate, while decreasing taxes for the well-to-do. They have no quarrel with spending your taxes on subsidies to wealthy corporations, high living and ever-larger government. They take our surplus Social Security money and spend it on current budget items to reduce the deficit, and then advocate cutting back on benefits and resist cost-of-living increases for retirees because "we can't afford it."

Dividends on Taxes

Even though an enormous amount of taxes are wasted, we have to recognize that a great deal of money is spent correctly. Without police and fire protection, highways, libraries, schools and health services, our lives would be very different. Without Medicare, Social Security and other programs for senior citizens, prospects for retirement would be indeed grim. Agreed, not all our tax money is spent on boondoggles. This brings us to the focus of this chapter: what government and private services are out there for senior citizens, and how to get your share.

"Wait a minute," I hear you saying, "some of those services sound like charity. Charity is for losers, not for me!" Well, perhaps some of this *sounds* like charity, but the cold fact is that you have paid for these services all your life. You've paid through taxes, club dues, United Way contributions and money in the Sunday collection plate. All these years, you've subsidized tasty meals at the local senior citizens center, paid for card tables and bridge prizes and home care for invalids. If you don't participate, it's like putting money in a bank and failing to take it out when you most need it. Now *that's* being a loser! It is of utmost importance that those forced to retire on limited budgets participate in these senior citizen services. It makes retirement on a shoestring much easier.

Food Stamp Eligibility

For some reason, many folks look down their noses at food stamps. They feel this is some kind of sleazy panhandling or charity. One reason for this negative impression of food stamps is the continual harping by certain political opportunists who see this as a way to increase their popularity with those voters who don't receive food stamps. The political hopefuls make it sound as if recipients are guilty of something or other when the government sells them the stamps which can be used for food.

The fact is, the food stamp money comes from the same Department of Agriculture funds that also go to wealthy farmers who receive huge checks for raising certain crops and for *not* growing others. Some of this money goes to pay subsidies to gentlemen farmers who grow tobacco for cigarettes and chewing tobacco. Huge corporate farms collect millions of dollars of government money, crop insurance and assistance of all kinds. Dairy farmers have received over $100,000,000 (some farmers over a million dollars apiece) to slaughter their animals so that the government wouldn't have to pay more money in subsidies and price supports, and taxpayers wouldn't have to buy the surplus cheese and store it in caves until it rots.

We seldom hear criticism about these Agriculture Department expenditures. But we hear plenty about "welfare queens" who drive Cadillacs and who buy groceries with food stamps. Well, it turns out that if a person owns an automobile that's worth more than $4,500, it is counted against the food stamp applicant as cash assets, which affects eligibility. So, don't become angry at some out-of-work housewife who happens to drive a beat-up old Caddy to the supermarket.

Food stamp eligibility requirements change with the Consumer Price Index, but at the end of 1991, they were as follows: A single person can have no more than $718 a month in gross income, and a couple no more than $962 per month. This includes Social Security payments. They can have no more than $2,000 in cash or assets that can be turned into cash (stocks, IRAs, etc.). If they are over 65, the maximum is $3,000. As you might guess, there is no maximum income or net worth restrictions on the tobacco farmers to be eligible for their payoffs.

A home is not counted as a cash asset, but an automobile is, as noted above, if it is worth over $4,500. There is a complicated formula for figuring just how much of the excess is counted as assets. An interesting note: a motorhome or RV is considered an asset if valued over $4,500, *unless* you live in it full time, when it is considered to be your home. If you live in your rig for only half of the year, it doesn't count as your home.

With the strict eligibility for qualifying for food stamps, the surprising thing is just how many folks in the United States are qualifying. Newspaper articles in the winter of 1991 stated that one out of ten citizens were receiving them! That's over 24 million people who are earning less than the maximum and who do not have assets over the prohibited amount! So, if you are not receiving food stamps, please do not look down on those who do. If you must be angry with someone, take it out on the wealthy farmers and the Department of Agriculture. Should you qualify, by all means, use your rights. You've already paid your share, and now it's your turn.

Medical Care U.S.A.

The United States is alone among the world of civilized nations in failing to provide adequate medical care for its citizens. Even most third-world nations see to it that their citizens do not die from lack of medical care; the life expectancy in the U.S. is now actually *lower* than some "backward" countries. Almost 300,000 times a year people are turned away from U.S. hospitals when they need care. Yes, there is such a thing as Medicare for those who qualify and Medicaid for the poor who do not qualify. But only 38 percent of the U.S. poor are covered by Medicaid and people on Medicare need extra private insurance to cover themselves adequately. Those too poor to afford medical insurance and those who make too much to get Medicaid are in deep trouble.

For people facing retirement, medical care is crucial, because one illness can totally wipe out the savings of a lifetime. While medical expenses rise at the rate of 10 to 20 percent a year, more and more are falling through that famous "safety net."

A growing concern over the disgraceful state of health care is forcing the Administration and Congress to make some half-hearted mumblings about "doing something about it." But don't try to hold off being sick until they do. There are too many powerful lobby interests against it. Insurance companies become hysterical at the thought of national health care as does the American Medical Association. This is the same AMA that in 1965 came out against Medicare, and also against the surgeon general's report which suggested that smoking causes cancer. It's not surprising that the AMA is staunchly opposed to national health care. I can't help but wonder if the concern is about health or about protecting doctors' incomes. The next time you write a letter to your congressman, mention health care.

Medicare

Medicare was a marvelous step forward, and a godsend for the elderly. But it was only one step forward (and it's had to struggle to keep from being pushed back by special interest groups). There are some holes in Medicare so it's important to know which gaps need to be covered by supplementary insurance. Your local Social Security office has several publications and pamphlets which describe in detail what you are entitled to; others are listed in the Appendix. Regulations change from time to time, so it's best to be abreast of the latest. I'll only attempt to give an overview here; you need to rely on your Medicare office and your local senior services agencies for up-to-date details.

Basically, there are two parts to Medicare: the Hospital Insurance (Part A) and the Medical Insurance (Part B). Generally, Part A coverage provides for the following items, but take note of the exceptions, the amounts *not* covered. Medicare pays all approved charges for the first 60 days of inpatient *hospital care* in a benefit period, after you pay the *first $628* of approved charges. (Should the doctor charge more than is approved, you pick up the tab.) For the 61st through the 90th day, Medicare pays all approved charges except for *$157 per day* which you pay. If you need more than 90 days of hospitalization in any benefit period, you have 60 *lifetime reserve days* which are not renewable; once you use them, they're gone. Each reserve day costs you *$314*. It also helps with 100 days of inpatient, post-hospital nursing facility care; Medicare pays for the first 20 days, then you pay *$78.50 a day* for the next 80 days. It pays all *approved charges* for medically necessary home health care. The catch here is what Medicare considers approved and what is not. Doctors often have different notions as to their worth than do Medicare officials. The bright side of this picture is: Medicare covers most of the costs if a doctor certifies you as terminally ill and you are sent to a hospice until you kick the bucket. That oughta cheer you up.

What is not covered? Medicare Plan A doesn't cover telephones or televisions, private rooms or private duty nurses, and it won't pay for staying in a nursing facility if it is mainly personal care, such as help in walking, getting in and out of bed, eating, dressing, bathing and taking medicine.

Medicare Part B Medical Insurance helps pay for doctor bills, outpatient hospital services (such as emergency room), ambulatory surgery, diagnostic tests, laboratory services and Pap smears. In addition it pays for physical, occupational and speech therapy services, and durable medical equipment and supplies. Medicare doesn't pay for *all* of these services, just 80 percent of approved charged. There's also a $100 deductible in addition to the remaining 20 percent of the bills. Many things are not covered, items such as eyeglasses, dentures, hearing aids or routine physical exams. Medicare helps cushion the blows of medical woes, but it's only a cushion, not a shield.

Medigap Insurance

As you can see, there are many holes in Medicare, holes which can suck up savings accounts in a hurry. Most people (who can afford it) purchase additional coverage, known as "Medigap," which is supposed to cover some or all of your extra medical costs. These come in the form of Medicare supplements and major medical policies. This has been a fertile field for con artists working for some unscrupulous insurance companies who high-pressure clients into buying more insurance than needed or policies that don't pay off as advertised. Be sure to order the free booklet, *Guide to Health Insurance for People with Medicare* (details in Appendix). And don't let a suede-shoes salesman scare you into a policy that isn't right for you.

Free Medicare?

According to the January 1992 issue of *Modern Maturity* (AARP's fine publication), more than two million Medicare beneficiaries are paying too much for their Part B premiums. As much as a thousand dollars a year too much! It seems there are some "secret benefits" intended for low income retirees; "secret" because the state governments are keeping it quiet and saving money by not fulfilling their obligations under law.

It turns out that in 1988 and again in 1990, Congress enacted a *Qualified Medicare Beneficiary program* (QMB), which requires states, through their Medicaid programs, to pay Part B premiums for those whose incomes are at or below the poverty level. In some instances they are supposed to pay co-payments and deductibles, that is if a patient qualifies, he or she isn't billed for some or all of the excluded charges. However, if you don't apply for this assistance, the state won't pay. They have no way of knowing your economic situation unless you speak up. And apparently they aren't asking, as one way of saving money.

There are other Medicare and Medicaid benefits which accrue to very low income patients. If you are in this category you should inquire at the Medicaid office of your local department of human welfare or social services. The local senior citizens center can supply you with directions. Should you have problems getting information, look in the phone book in the government section, and look for your state or local Area Agency on Aging office. For a pamphlet describing eligibility, an application and other detailed information, send a self-addressed stamped envelope to Families USA, 1334 G St. NW, Washington, DC 20005. See Bibliography for other Medicare publications available free of charge from the government.

Social Security Disability

You don't have to be 62 or over to draw Social Security if you should become disabled or blind. The key to this is when a doctor or doctors certify that you are "totally and permanently disabled for a period of not less than one year." Because many people have faked disabilities in the past, the Social Security Administration takes a hard look at each case, and will disallow all but the most obvious disabilities. If you feel that you are truly disabled, by all means, appeal the decision. You don't have to have an attorney for an appeal, but should you decide that you want one, most will work on contingency (if you get nothing, they charge nothing.)

SSI Supplement

Supplementary Security Income (SSI for short) pays monthly checks to some who aren't entitled to regular Social Security. To qualify you must be 65 or older or disabled or blind, and you must have little or no income. It's important to note that SSI isn't just for elderly, it can be paid at any age as long as the applicant meets the above standards. Blind doesn't necessarily mean totally blind, very poor vision will sometimes qualify you. Disabled doesn't mean confined to a wheelchair; if doctors agree that you have a physical or mental problem that keeps you from working and is expected to last at least a year or to result in death, you may qualify.

The basic SSI check is $407 for a single person and $610 a month for a couple (in 1991). Some states add money to that amount. In addition, folks who qualify for SSI usually also qualify for Medicaid and food stamps.

The financial qualifications vary from state to state but basically, your total income must be less than $427 for one person and $630 as a couple. There are some items of income that don't count. For example: the first $65 of your earnings every month, food stamps, food, clothing or shelter from private non-profit organizations and most home energy assistance. There are other exemptions, which your local welfare office can explain. You cannot have assets that exceed $2,000 for singles or $3,000 for couples. Again, there are some assets that are exempt, which will be explained when you make application.

Senior Citizens Services

Some communities have fantastically successful programs that can make a world of difference in people's lives. Many retired folks make the local senior center their focal point, taking advantage of free medical services, nutritious meals, as well as social activities and a host of other free benefits. Senior citizen centers help make shoestring retirement possible.

The surprising thing about these community services is that so few retirees take full advantage of them. Recently, when doing research at a particularly attractive senior center, we asked the director what she considered to be her biggest problem. She replied, "Getting the news out that we exist! Folks just have no idea of what we offer. We send out mailings and we ask our people to spread the word among their low-income neighbors. Many of our services are free, some have a nominal cost, others have a sliding fee, according to the ability to pay. Some items are limited to lower-income folks, but most are available to all. Yet, we can't seem to spread the news!"

She then began listing the things senior citizens are entitled to in her area, most of them just for the asking:

Adult day care. Hourly out-of-home day care to provide respite care or daily care when needed. This is a life-saver for a spouse who is tied down with taking care of his or her partner. It provides a chance to go shopping or enjoy a movie or some outside recreation without having to worry about the partner.

Adult family homes. Room and board in a licensed residential environment for the senior requiring some assistance with daily living tasks. For the single person who hasn't the resources or the resignation to go to a "nursing home."

Adult protective services/elder abuse. This provides investigation of abuse, neglect, exploitation or abandonment, and short-term emergency support to adults in need of protection.

Advocacy program. Volunteers provide assistance for low-income seniors to cut through red tape. They receive help with forms, applications and appeals plus advice on how to handle bureaucracy. Free civil legal services by volunteer attorneys are available to eligible, low-income clients. No child custody, criminal or litigation cases are accepted.

Alzheimers support group. Provides counseling, information and support for families. Very important for those frustrated by an inability to get help.

Blind or impaired vision services. Offers a variety of services to blind of all ages. "Talking" books are featured as a part of this program.

Blood pressure checks. Free monitoring of blood pressure is provided by volunteers.

Chore and in-home care service. Assistance with household tasks, shopping, meal preparation, personal care and transportation to medical appointments. Sliding fees make it affordable and help keep folks out of expensive health-care institutions.

Clothing bank. Provides suitable clothing for senior citizens. Donations come from closets of well-off members of the community, so the quality of the clothing is very good.

Dental care access. This program provides low-income seniors with reduced cost dental care.

Educational opportunities. A variety of classes are available to seniors free or for a minimal fee. In addition to educational classes, classes such as aerobics, art, health and nutrition, water exercise and driver's ed are offered.

Employment. A special program for seniors, with on-the-job training, part-time employment and job-search assistance.

Financial assistance. Information and support concerning Medicaid assistance for low-income seniors, Social Security problems and general financial assistance for low-income aged, disabled and/or blind individuals.

Food bank. Gives food to elderly in need or in emergency situations. Some of the food comes from government surplus commodities, some from donations by local businesses, the rest from community funds. USDA food surplus and donated food is distributed to needy low-income people

Food stamps. Help in receiving coupons for expanding the ability to purchase food for low-income individuals.

Health care. Immunizations, screening for diabetes, hearing and blood pressure. A tuberculosis clinic and a low-cost program of foot-care clinics are located throughout the county. Financial assistance is available for those in need of a hearing aid.

Home delivered meals. Famous Meals-on-Wheels for home-bound seniors over 60. A donation of $1.50 per meal is suggested, but only if the person can afford it. Care is taken not to embarrass those who cannot pay.

Home health care. Skilled nurses visit the home, as well as physical therapists. This is covered either by Medicare, Medicaid, private insurance, or on a sliding fee scale for low-income people.

Hospice program. Provides education and emotional support for the terminally ill and their families. In this case, Hospice works to enable the patient to stay in his or her own home.

Legal services. Free legal services to older persons regarding their civil rights, benefits, entitlements. Reduced fees for simple wills and community property agreements.

Low rent housing. In this particular town there were over 300 units, ranging from efficiencies to small houses, that were managed by the county Housing Authority. They were limited to low-income senior adults aged 62 or more or senior couples (at least one 62 or more). There was a waiting list for vacancies at the moment. Mortgage assistance was also available.

Medical equipment is available for loan to eligible individuals.

Nutrition. Lunches for seniors served at noon Monday through Friday. The suggested donation of $1.50 is not expected of those who cannot afford it. Also, as previously mentioned, hot meals are sent to home-bound seniors through the Meals-on-Wheels program.

Recreation is provided at all of the senior centers in the area. Arts and crafts, card games, poker, dances and any number of recreational programs limited only by their imagination.

Transportation. Door-to-door transportation for eligible seniors takes them shopping, to libraries and on errands. Volunteers provide transportation to doctors offices, therapy sessions and to hospitals.

There's More!

Other services we've found in some communities are:

Adopt-A-Senior program. Volunteers provide socialization and transportation assistance for those who are socially or geographically isolated and need assistance to meet daily living needs.

Companion program. Volunteers provide social contact and support for elderly persons who show signs of confusion or weakness. Services as shopping, visiting, running errands and brief respite are available.

Guardianship. Program provides advocacy services for those who are no longer able to make decisions or access essential services for themselves.

Emergency rent assistance. Provides help for low income elderly when an eviction notice has been served and when all other state and local resources have been exhausted.

Energy assistance. This program informs seniors about utility discounts and rebates to which they are entitled, and administers a federally funded program designed to assist low income households during the winter months. Helps pay heating bills and assists homebound in completing applications.

Senior travel club. Day trips, overnight getaways and longer excursions are provided at very low cost.

Telephone reassurance program. Provides regular connections with a volunteer caller, who talks with home-bound seniors at pre-arranged daily times. This helps many invalids live independently, and gives them confidence that someone in the community cares about their well-being. There are no fees for this service.

Transportation services. Some communities have wheelchair lift vans available by appointment for door-to-door transportation. Buses and vans running fixed routes to hospitals, clinics, dialysis services and other medical facilities are also common. Another aid is door-to-door escort service for trips to doctors, shopping and other necessary trips.

All Are Not Equally Good

The senior citizen program described above is a splendid example of a community in action, providing quality services for its retired and elderly citizens. But be aware that not all organizations operate in the same manner. Before making a decision on where to retire, a visit to the local senior citizens center is highly advisable. Talk to the director and staff and see what is provided and the spirit in which it is provided.

During our research, we were continually surprised at the wide differences between senior centers in the towns we visited around the country. In some places the levels of interest and quality of services were even higher—in others, next to nothing was available. The lesson is: All senior citizen centers are not equal.

For example: one center we visited served free coffee and doughnuts in the morning while arts and crafts programs were getting underway, as well as soft drinks in the evening at dances and card parties. Daily meals were delicious and tastefully served, with cooking done on premises by a staff of paid senior citizen workers. At least ten rooms were devoted to different activities, including a library, conference and exercise rooms. Hundreds of enthusiastic senior citizens worked on volunteer, self-help programs while city, county and federal government funds paved the way for success.

Another center, in a similar-sized town, consisted of nothing more than a small, single room with a couple of shabby card tables. The door was open for just a few hours every afternoon, mostly for poker games. As for meals, we were told that two churches served lunch—one day a week each—and the local Elks Club and Lions Club also provided lunch one day apiece, making a total of four meals during the week. Nothing was provided by the center itself. But, in addition to being away from the intimacy of "their own" center, an automobile was required to get to the meals, and they had the unmistakable aroma of charity. Instead of enthusiastic, caring staff members, we found one manager who seemed to resent our taking up her time with an interview.

It's There for You

For senior citizens on limited budgets, these services can make the difference between making out nicely or having to scrimp by. The inexpensive (or free) meals served at the senior centers are often not only nutritious and tasty, but also served in a pleasant setting where you can visit with friends and make new ones.

If, God forbid, you have health problems, in-home care employees will perform household tasks necessary to keep you in a clean, safe environment. They will prepare meals, vacuum, change linens, do laundry, mop floors and clean sinks. In addition, they provide transportation and/or escorting to all types of medical services when public transit isn't available, even doing shopping and running errands when necessary. In-home care programs mean being able to remain at home during convalescence instead of being forced into expensive care facilities not covered by Medicare. These programs are funded by federal, state and local tax monies. Most of these programs aren't limited to low-income senior citizens, by the way. All ranges of income are eligible, although higher-income persons are sometimes required to contribute toward the service cost based on a sliding fee scale.

An additional benefit, of interest to those senior citizens who are in need of part-time work, is that the paid in-home care employees are often senior citizens.

Volunteering

The most successful and energetic senior citizen centers all seem to have one thing in common: a large number of volunteers. Folks at these centers with high levels of services don't just sit back and wait for things to happen, or for the government to do something for them; they get out and *make* things happen! Their enthusiasm is catching. It spreads to local officials, to local citizens and businesses, bringing everybody into the act. They get involved in local politics and let their voices and needs be known. (Politicians listen when voters speak.)

Therefore, the best way to help yourself in a senior citizen center is to volunteer and help others. I've discussed this in an earlier chapter, but it cannot be stressed too strongly. By volunteering, you gain a deeper sense of self-respect and sense of well-being, and you build up a debt of gratitude which may well be repaid someday—when you need it most. Somewhere down the line, you will need help, and you will feel free to call in your debts.

Often, volunteer jobs have a way of working into paid positions. Always, you will widen your network of friends. And finally, you'll know that you aren't receiving charity, because you are giving just as much as you are receiving.

Sharing Experience of a Lifetime

This is the motto of RSVP (Retired Senior Volunteer Program), one of the most exciting volunteer programs of all. Funded by the United Way Agency and other community and governmental funds, this volunteer program channels the talents and experiences of its members into invaluable service. Because of its flexibility, RSVP finds ways to utilize each volunteer's individual needs, interests and physical capabilities to the best interests of the community. There is no charge for their services.

Whenever you find a strong, active RSVP, you can be pretty sure of also finding dynamic and valuable services for senior citizens. On any given day, RSVP volunteers are found in schools, libraries, nursing homes, hospitals and many non-profit organizations. RSVP volunteers are especially helpful in providing respite service for families with problems such as stroke, Alzheimer's, Parkinson's, cancer, cardiac or respiratory diseases.

Newspaper Resources

Every community seems to have at least one senior citizen newspaper. These are valuable sources of information about what is going on in the community and what services are available for the asking. Not all of the help comes from federal, state and local government; many services are donated by charitable organizations, corporations and private enterprises.

At random I pick up an issue of a senior citizen newspaper from the tall stack of publications that we've collected in our travels. This happens to be a very non-commercial looking publication; much of it appears to be typewritten (possibly produced by volunteer labor)—and it is chock full of interesting information. In addition to chatty local news, this paper furnished its readers with the following information:

1. The fact that low income housing applications are being accepted, plus the addresses and telephone numbers of the agencies who can help place senior citizens in affordable housing.

2. A free legal seminar, in which an attorney will cover the subject of wills, the "right to die" and other matters of interest to retirees.

3. A list of senior citizen centers serving noon meals, and the menus for the week at each center. (They look tasty!)

4. A notice that the local college is sponsoring an Elderhostel Program with some highly interesting classes. The important part of the announcement is that folks over 60, with a yearly income of less than $12,000, can attend the classes for only $50 a week, including tuition, room and meals!

5. A warning from the state insurance commissioner that many senior citizens are paying too much for Medicare premiums and deductibles—often $1,000 a year to much. He gives information on how to cut these overpayments.

6. Comprehensive guidelines for choosing a good nursing home. Ways to determine whether you will be happy there and whether the staff and management truly care about the patients over profits.

7. A list of volunteer opportunities through RSVP, including such diverse jobs as helping with a Kid Town fair, being a guide at a museum and blacksmith shop, as well as working at a disabled children's center.

8. A complete directory of community services, including health, legal, transportation and the full spectrum of help available to senior citizens for Alzheimer sufferers, lung problems, a stroke patients' support group, home delivered meals, plus a dozen other programs.

9. A list of community activities with a calendar listing potlucks, quilting classes, blood pressure clinics, exercise classes, pinochle games, dancing, senior singles clubs, senior softball games and much more. There were even free podiatry checkups for those who wear their feet out trying to attend all of these activities.

10. The monthly listing of the Senior Travel Club, which makes inexpensive trips to nearby tourist attractions, sometimes overnight, sometimes day trips.

Of further interest were the free classified advertisements. Readers offered to do house cleaning, to sell fishing rods, bandsaws and three-wheel motorscooters. One individual offered to sell a "complete cremation package, including transfer and storage of remains. $2,000 value discounted 50% for cash or trade for firearms of equal value."

Even though you probably aren't particularly interested in buying a second-hand cremation package, these local Senior newspapers can put you in touch with what's happening in the community. You'll know whether you're getting your share of the benefits you used to provide for the elderly. Now it's your turn! (Now why would anybody want to trade a perfectly good cremation package for weapons???)

Chapter Four

Working and Retirement

Work begins the day we enter kindergarten. That's when our on-the-job training begins (without pay, of course). We quickly learn that we have a solid obligation to get up every morning—whether we want to or not—and that we must appear at a certain place at a certain time. We discover that we have a "boss" (the teacher) and we must please the boss if life is going to be tolerable. Until each long, wearisome school day draws to a merciful close, teachers and administrators direct our souls, control our lives and limit our leisure time. I'm convinced that the fourth grade is the longest period of time ever measured.

By the time we finally finish school and enter the job market, we've learned our lessons well. Get up every day, go somewhere, perform work we may or may not enjoy, and be rewarded with a weekly paycheck instead of a report card. Weekends off, plus a two-week vacation, are the only respite from the grinding schedule. To miss a day's work means losing a day's pay—a serious blow to many budgets—so we go to work even though we feel terrible. Missing too many days work means losing a job—a disaster.

This process, started in kindergarten, is relentlessly reinforced through the next sixty years our lives. We suffer from a mental hang-up called the "work ethic." To have a job is good. Not to have a job is bad. To lose a job is ruinous. Only bums live without working.

Suddenly—willingly or not—you stumble into retirement. You no longer have a job, a boss to please or a place to be every day at a specified hour—or else. You can get up when you please, take a nap when you please and you don't have to please anyone who doesn't please you.

For some people, this is a wonderful situation: the goal they've worked for and anticipated since that first day in kindergarten. School's out! Vacation from now on!

But for many others, retirement is a terrible shock. There's something wicked or evil about breaking this pattern of responsibility to a job. When one of these individuals wakes up in the morning without a job to go to, a feeling of guilt sets in. "Something is terribly wrong here," the person thinks, "I should be working, suffering, making money..."

This guilty feeling is why many folks refuse to retire, even though they work at jobs they hate. Others, when forced into retirement, insist on finding full-time or part-time jobs, whether they need the money or not. To me, this seems like a tragic waste of a lifetime's goal.

Retirement shouldn't mean dropping out of the world, and it doesn't necessarily mean the end of a person's working career. On the contrary, for most folks retirement means the chance to do what they *want* to do rather than what they *have* to do. You now have the time to write a book, join an actor's group, become a fishing guide or turn your hobby into a profitable occupation. This may be the time to take up a new hobby, to explore an unlimited range of options. Learn to feel sorry for those who still have to work instead of feeling guilty for not being with them.

For those who need to be "doing something" but who can get by without extra income, our recommendation is volunteer work. As a volunteer, you will not only be doing something meaningful and worthwhile, but you meet other volunteers in your community, widen your network of friends and lay the groundwork for later years when you may need volunteers to help *you*.

On the other hand, there are those who unquestionably need extra earnings to supplement their Social Security or other pension income. Part-time or full-time jobs can mean the difference between bare survival and a comfortable retirement. Yet, sometimes the income earned can be costly—in several ways.

Expensive Jobs

One way a job can cost money is the government's attitude toward working while drawing Social Security. To discourage retirees from earning money, the government subtracts $1.00 for every $2.00 you earn over a specified amount (depending upon the age at which you retired). In 1991, at age 62, a retiree was permitted to earn $7,080 before having to pay back half of the excess.

Let's take the case of Roger, a commercial printer who lost his $16-an-hour job because desktop publishing put his employer out of business. Since he was 62 years old, Roger applied for Social Security and was entitled to $768 a month (amounting to $9,216 a year or $177 a week). Finding he needed more income, he looked for a job. The best he could find paid $6.45 an hour ($258 a week). Better than nothing, he thought. Before long, he discovered that he had to repay $3,168 of his Social Security money because at $6.45 an hour he earned too much money! For full-time employment, Roger was only entitled to make $3.40 an hour without penalty—not even minimum wage. In other words, Roger was working the first ten hours of every week for nothing—just to make up for the money deducted from his Social Security! To add insult to injury, he had to pay taxes on the excess $3,168. He immediately started looking for a *part-time* job.

Good Jobs and High Prices

Part-time work is the solution for many starvation budgets. The problem is that competition for these jobs can be fierce and pay can be very low. This is the dilemma: where part-time jobs are plentiful and pay is good, you'll find the cost-of-living impossible. A booming economy brings high rents, costly utility bills and elevated living costs as well as high wages. It doesn't make good sense to retire where living costs are exorbitant, in order to find a good-paying part-time job, in order to be able to afford the extra expenses of retiring in a costly area. You're right back where you started.

I have a friend who lived in a nice apartment in Monterey, California. Her rent was $700 a month. The high cost of living in Monterey wouldn't permit her to live on Social Security. She found a part-time job in a bookstore that paid $6.00 an hour ($400 a month clear) for working five afternoons a week (20 hours). If she earned more than this, she would start losing Social Security benefits. When she decided to move to a smaller town in a lower-cost area, she found an equally nice apartment for $300 a month. Part-time jobs there paid about $4.50 an hour, but no jobs were available. At first she was disappointed—until she realized that the $400 she saved in rent made up for the $400 she had been earning at her bookstore job. In other words, she had been going to work five afternoons a week just to pay higher rent. Now she devotes her time to very satisfying volunteer work in the community.

Finding Retirement Jobs

Some retirees have lifetime job skills that make it relatively easy to find part-time work. Even though they no longer have the strength and stamina to handle some of the tougher jobs, their experience and good judgment qualify them for consulting and/or supervisory work. Nurses, secretaries, bookkeepers and others with rich work backgrounds find themselves in great demand, if only for vacation fill-ins.

Not everybody has these levels of competency at a trade or profession, so it might appear more difficult to find part-time work. However, just about everyone has something valuable to contribute to the job market, if it's just enthusiasm and a willingness to work.

The Yellow Pages of your telephone directory will list several temporary employment firms, such as Manpower or Kelly (used to be Kelly *Girls*, remember?). They are nearly always in need of temporary or seasonal workers, and can usually be depended on to find a job when needed. These jobs have a way of becoming a regular thing when the employer is pleased with a worker's performance. The good thing about these situations is that it's understood from the beginning that they are temporary, so you aren't in an embarrassing position if you quit after you've earned as much as permitted.

Another way to look for jobs is to inquire at the local senior citizens' center. They can direct you to a Senior Citizen Council office (if it isn't in the center itself) where the staff works at placing senior citizens in both permanent and temporary jobs. Of course, the newspaper's "help-wanted" classified pages carry employment opportunities, but many prefer younger applicants. By placing your own ad in the "situation-wanted" column, you can put forward your own unique qualifications, job requirements and special preferences. If you have special skills that might be attractive to a particular group of employers, the telephone book will provide a mail list for you to send a resume. As a final resort, there's always the state employment bureau, or human development department—whatever it calls itself. There, however, you are competing with unemployed workers who are looking for jobs while collecting unemployment benefits.

In Chapter Six we discuss ways full-time RVers find jobs. Many of the same principles apply to non-RV folks. For example, the *Workamper News*, a newsletter directed toward full-time RV travelers, lists many jobs where the employers not only provide paid jobs, but free room and board as well.

Sales Work

For the outgoing personality, one of the easiest jobs to find are in commission sales. The reason is obvious: the employer has no salaries or benefits to pay until you sell something. Automobile agencies typically have half a dozen salespersons lounging about in hopes that a buyer will happen along. Real estate offices can afford to have large staffs because they don't pay wages. Often, the salesperson is obligated to spend some time taking care of the office (at no pay) in addition to sales work. There are many other businesses that offer very little in the way of wages, expecting the employees to earn the rest of their income from commissions. When successful, these jobs make good part-time occupations, and often pay very well. The down side is, when things aren't selling, you not only get nothing for your time, but it can also be excruciatingly boring.

Another sales situation is with multi-level products wherein commissions are paid partly to the salesperson and some goes up to the salesperson who recruited him or her...and so on. I'm not sure these ever work. I do know that there are a couple of Amway products that I truly like better than anything else I've found. Yet, while I can always find people wanting me to become a distributor and *sell* Amway products for *them*, they seldom seem interested in selling *me* the products I need.

Starting Your Own Business

Before you think of starting a home business, you need to examine your own personality, to ask yourself some questions and supply some honest answers. From the book *Starting a Mini-Business, a Guidebook for Seniors*, 1988, (by Nancy Olsen, Fair Oaks Publishing Co., Sunnyvale CA), comes some of the following ideas on this subject. Ask yourself these questions.

1. *Are you a self-starter?* If you are one of those who hate getting up in the morning and getting after business, being your own boss won't be any fun.

2. *How do you feel about dealing with people?* You need to like working with people if you are going to get into your own business. Almost all types of business requires daily contact with others.

3. *Can you take responsibility?* Are you the type who can forge ahead and get things done, or have you always expected others to do things for you?

4. *How good an organizer are you?* Running a business means being organized. You're going to have to keep books, records, and keep your fingers on all the strings.

5. *Can you make decisions?* At every turn in the road, there are going to be instant choices to be made. If you can't, you're going to be paralyzed. Your business will suffer.

6. *Can you stick with it?* You can't always expect to make money from the very beginning. If you don't encounter instant success, are you going to become discouraged before your enterprise gets the chance to fly?

7. *How good is your health?* Will you truly have the energy to follow through on your business.

If after analyzing yourself, you are still assured that you really want to go into business, you might check with the office of the U.S. Small Business Administration. There are 100 offices in cities nationwide, offering free counseling, literature and sometimes financial assistance for starting a business.

Beware of Fancy Advertisements

Magazines are liberally sprinkled with ads urging you to start your own business, and the advertiser offers to help you get started

If you've been around long enough to think about retirement, you've also got the smarts to know these things are too good to be true. The ads claim you can make $100 an hour cleaning carpets, selling stationery or some other scheme, but you end up paying lots of money for nothing. Local newspaper ads can sometimes be phony as well. I had a friend who answered an ad that offered to set up applicants with a free delivery route business, stocking supermarkets with a nationally known product. He should have known there was something wrong when the company insisted that he buy an expensive delivery van from them—at their price—and when the company "union" demanded a huge initiation fee. It turned out that the union and company were splitting the initiation fees and down payments, and the new "employees" were laid off when new applicants came up with more money. They terminated the job but not the payments on the van. Oh well, he was able to use the van for camping and eventually drove his money's worth out of it.

The Whole Work Catalog

A well-stocked bookstore will have several books on how to find jobs and how to start your own business. A mail order company called The New Careers Center, in Boulder, Colorado, has a full collection of these kinds of books. They cover subjects such as finding jobs with a cruise line, teaching English abroad, jobs in national parks, starting a business in your own home and freelancing opportunities. Don't expect to find many astounding secrets for making money, but these books could be the source of new ideas on work opportunities.

Some of the titles are: *Moonlighting: 148 Great Ways to Make Money on the Side*; the *Work-at-Home Sourcebook* and *Starting a Mini-Business: A Guidebook for Seniors* (mentioned above). Write and ask for *The Whole Work Catalog*, New Careers Center, P.O. Box 339-CT, Boulder, CO 80306.

Be aware that how-to-do-it schemes on earning lots of money at home can be overly optimistic, to say the least. Don't pin your future on a flowery magazine advertisement assuring you that you can make $100,000 a year in your spare time. One example I am familiar with is books claiming to have the secrets of making a good living by travel or other freelance writing. As a long-time freelancer, I can assure you that I would have starved long ago had I depended upon travel or feature articles for food on the table. What self-help books don't tell you is that newspapers have access to tons of articles and feature material from syndicated wire services—for free. Unless you have something of special interest to local readers, newspapers would be wasting money; they already have more free material than they could possibly use. The few papers that do use freelancers often have such a small budget for outside material that it's hardly worth the postage. Successful magazines usually employ staff writers, and run-of-the-mill publications often pay no better than newspapers, and sometimes not at all. They feel that a byline is sufficient reward.

That's not to say there are not rewards in freelance writing. The rewards come in the form of satisfaction in being published, in ego gratification and an occasional freebie from a business looking for publicity. With notable exceptions, the small checks place most freelancing in the category of a hobby rather than a business.

Underground Economy

The Internal Revenue Service is deeply concerned with what it calls the "underground economy." Throughout the country, folks are dealing with each other in cash transactions—or trading goods and services which amount to income—yet they neglect to report these transactions on their income tax forms.

For example: if you do housework for someone in exchange for reduced rent, you should report the rent as wage income while the landlord reports your labor as rental income. If you sell items at a flea market, you are supposed to report your profits. I don't know if it's ever happened, but that's the way it's *supposed* to be. Since there is no "paper trail" of transactions, and since the individual amounts are relatively insignificant, the IRS finds it almost impossible to catch these small-time tax evaders. The IRS seems genuinely surprised and indignant over these transgressions, and estimates that if everyone paid income tax on their earnings there would be additional billions pouring into our national coffers every year. On the other hand, if the wealthy were limited in their loopholes, the amount of additional revenue would be staggering. (The IRS seldom mentions this little problem.)

Part-time Instructors

There are many ways of taking advantage of your life experience. In the October 1990 issue of *Trailer Life*, Buck Buchanan wrote about short-term teaching jobs in trade schools that often go begging for instructors. The problem can be especially critical in smaller towns where qualified craftsmen forsake the lower wages offered there and head for the bigger cities. The essential requirements are not necessarily a college degree, but a solid knowledge of your craft, and the ability to pass this knowledge on. Even in states and localities where academic qualifications are strict for community college and trade schools, Adult Education instructors do not always have to match the formal requirements required of regular instructors. I once volunteered to work as a teacher's aide in an English-for-foreigners section of the local adult education program. When I tried to quit my volunteer position, the school begged me to stay, and put me on a paid basis. Before long, they made me a regular job and granted me a lifetime teaching credential as an English teacher in California's school system. All I really wanted to do was have fun helping foreigners learn to speak our language.

Teaching opportunities are often advertised in the local newspaper help-wanted classifieds. A phone call to the school department, especially to the Adult Education office, will verify whether there are any openings. If they don't have anything available, they surely know where to refer you. Some departments will actually create a class to fit an instructor's skills. If they can locate 15 or 20 students who are interested in your specialty, the school will receive money from the state to fund the class and pay your salary. It's best to prepare a resumé, detailing your work experience and what aspects of this experience you are capable of teaching. If you have some college credits, don't fail to mention them.

Many school districts find themselves faced with a shortage of substitute teachers for regular grade school and high school classes (partly because of the low pay scales for substitutes). If you have at least a bachelors degree, many schools are eager to put you on their list, even though you have no teaching credential. Classroom assistant jobs, almost always part-time, are also possibilities for those with any experience, and sometimes for those with no experience. Starting off as a volunteer is an excellent way to break in. Private schools don't usually have to demand state teaching credentials, and because their regular salaries are often lower, have difficulty obtaining teachers. Again, if you have some formal education, and feel qualified to teach a subject, you might consider a part-time position in a private school.

Chapter Five

Weather and Crime

Many people, when they think of retirement, conjure up visions of living in a warm climate, someplace where they'll not have to shovel snow or change to special tires for the winter. Perhaps they manage to spend a week or two of their precious vacation time in Phoenix or Miami during the dead of winter. Expensive, but worth it for many folks.

Finding a job in a warm climate isn't usually a practical alternative. The problem is, when too many others also move to those desirable climates, job competition becomes intense. Working conditions and wages can be substandard. More often than not, it's better to stay where you are until retirement.

But when that looked-forward-to day finally arrives, unless retirees have a more-than-adequate retirement income, most abandon that dream of Florida, Arizona or California retirement. They remember those expensive vacation interludes. They read in newspapers and magazines that these places are super-expensive. "I can't afford that," they say, as they make plans on toughing it out every winter for the rest of their lives.

If they were to consider the facts carefully, they would discover that suffering cold weather isn't necessary after all. The interesting thing is: some of the most reasonable living costs in the country are found in the some of most benign climates.

Several factors combine to make this true. For one thing, heating cost are obviously much lower in warmer climates. Furthermore, low wages are meaningless to a retiree who doesn't have to work any more; it doesn't matter if your neighbors earn lower wages than you used to make. On the contrary, smaller paychecks are a major factor in keeping prices down. When incomes fall below the national average, the cost of living follows suit.

One more cost-cutting condition: a wave of overbuilding during the easy S&L money era of the 1980s—in warm places like Florida, California and Arizona—has created a buyer's market in real estate, with rental vacancy rates high. While you might pay $600 a month for an apartment in Dayton, you could be spending $300 for the same quality in Daytona Beach. That gives you $300 to put toward groceries and the electric bill. This saving, alone, is reason enough to pull up stakes from a frigid winter zone. (If you can get the stakes out of the ground.)

This isn't true *everywhere* in the warm climates. The same pleasant weather that draws ordinary working people quite naturally brings in the big money as well. Places like Palm Beach, Scottsdale and Palm Springs aren't exactly places where you might expect to live on a shoestring. Yet, there are other places, not too far from these luxury neighborhoods where prices are reasonable, where living without snow shovels is possible on a restricted budget.

Saving on Utilities

If you live in a cold climate, you don't have to be reminded how much it costs to heat a home in the winter. We've talked to many couples who commonly spend over $250 a month heating their homes in the winter. Now, in some sections of the country, $250 can rent an adequate apartment or a small house, or it can buy groceries for an entire month. Yet there are places where you can avoid heating costs in all but the coolest weeks of the winter. We've interviewed folks who never pay more than $50 for utilities the year around, usually far less than that except for January and February. This means a savings of $200 a month on utilities. Add that $200 a month to the $300 a month you've saved on rent, and you are bringing your budget down to the point where you now have money to spend on yourself instead of blowing it on your home and its greedy furnace.

Okay, I hear you protesting, "But what about air conditioning in the summer? If I move to a warm climate, and if I spend as much to cool my house in the summer as I used to for heating in the winter, where are the savings!"

The point is: many families in the northern and midwestern states are hit with a double whammy. Winter temperatures dip below zero as often as summer days climb above 100 degrees. They spend as much on air conditioning in the summer as they do on heating in the winter! We have friends in St. Louis whose electric bills in the summer regularly top $200 a month. They find no relief from high utility costs in either season. However, as you will see later on, there are inexpensive places to live in this country where air conditioning is non-existent and heating systems are limited to plug-in space heaters.

Do You *Need* Air Conditioning?

Air conditioning is a wonderful invention, something that many people cannot conceive of doing without. Yet, think back a few years—when we were kids—nobody had air conditioning, did they? Yet we survived just fine. Remember when the only air conditioned building in town was the local movie theater? Remember those signs painted like icicles on the movie marquee that announced "air cooled inside"? In the "good old days," when thermometers topped ninety degrees, our parents used to string a hammock in the shade, relax and sip a cool lemonade or iced tea. Temperatures today haven't changed; unless there is some medical condition to the contrary, you seldom *have* to turn on the air conditioner.

On the other hand, when below-zero temperatures settle in for the winter, you don't have the option of lighting the furnace or not. If you don't, you die. Winter heating is a matter of life and death, whereas summer air conditioning is a matter of relative comfort.

If you hate the thought of hot summers, yet still want no-frost winters, there are many places in the country (mostly on the West Coast) where air conditioning is unknown. While writing this book, we are living in a California coastal town. None of the houses have air-conditioning because it never gets hot. When temperatures climb out of the 70s, the local newspaper announces the event with banner headlines. Our electric blanket goes on every night of the year without exception. On the other hand, in the dead of winter, should temperature fall low enough for frost to damage our jade plants or fuchsias, you can be sure of more banner headlines. As a matter of fact, we don't even *have* a furnace; a single gas space heater takes the chill off our large, two-bedroom apartment. There are hundreds of similar locations throughout

California, Oregon and Washington. The best part is, many of them are very affordable, among the lowest costs of living in the country, with real estate prices approaching rock-bottom. We've talked to folks who never spend over $30 a month on utilities.

In my neighborhood, it's shirtsleeve weather in the afternoons, but sweaters after dark, all year around. Nobody here owns an overcoat; when it's necessary to travel east in the winter, we have to scout around for one we can borrow. But many people love hot weather. They don't want to miss the experience of a real summer—with backyard barbecues; good, honest sunshine that makes a cold drink sound like heaven and balmy evenings that invite a dip in the swimming pool. They might not be happy where I live.

The Perfect Climate

Everyone seems to have a different definition of what is a "perfect climate," but the truth is, there is no such thing. Folks in Maine love their summers, but complain that winters are cold and dreary. Their neighbors who retired in Florida adore Miami winters, but complain because summers are too muggy. Hawaii has near-perfect weather, but you'd better take a shopping bag full of money if you expect to stay very long. The nice thing about retirement, you have a variety of choices about your weather.

Personally, I consider parts of *inland* California, Oregon and Washington to have the best overall climate in the nation—sunny summers, with low humidity and relatively free of bugs. (I don't think I've ever seen a cockroach there.) Winter days require nothing more than a sweater or windbreaker, with little frost or snow—sometimes never. To illustrate how ill-prepared residents are for cold weather: in the winter of 1990 in Grants Pass, Oregon, an unusual cold snap burst water pipes throughout the area. Grants Pass residents do not customarily protect the pipes from freezing weather because cold snaps are so rare that it isn't worth the bother. But when I lived in Michigan, we wrapped exposed pipes in insulation and used electric warmers—or else.

Cold Weather Robbery

Readers will have little trouble detecting a definite bias in my writing, a bias against winter ice, dirty snow and slush. I fully realize that not everybody is trying to escape snow shovels. Many folks sincerely enjoy winters, with ice fishing, skiing and lovely Christmas card scenery. Therefore, I'll try to be careful not to make this book sound like a Chamber of Commerce advertisement for Florida or Arizona. But the facts are that cold weather can be very detrimental to your pocketbook—in many ways other than just heating bills or the extra wardrobe required for cold weather, with down jackets, padded boots and long underwear adding to the seasonal expenses. Clothing is a small consideration compared to other items, because clothing lasts for many seasons.

One unrecognized cost of cold weather is the subtle destruction of your automobile. Batteries deteriorate quickly in cold weather. Cold-weather starts wear out engine cylinders by dragging moving parts against each other without the benefit of free-flowing oil for lubrication. Antifreeze and snow tires also batter away at the budget. Unlike winter clothing, auto repair and maintenance are ongoing expenses which cannot be put off until next year.

The truly vicious damage comes from the effects of road salt. If you live where roads must be salted to clear away ice and snow you must deduct years from the useful life of your car. Salt destroys steel and body sheet metal faster than termites could ever attack a house! It's interesting to note that in the colder parts of the nation, regular leaded gasoline is generally unavailable. Yet, in Arizona, California and other dry climates, almost all service stations sell regular leaded gas. That's because older cars—the ones that burn old-fashioned leaded fuel—have long ago dissolved in the salt solutions that slosh around the roads in the winter climates. When you move to a salt-free environment, the life expectancy of your car depends on the number of *miles* you drive, not on the number of *winters* you survive. In short, salt will totally trash a car long before its warm-weather life expectancy.

Climate, Exercise and Health.

The other way cold weather can be costly is in terms of doctor bills and shortening of your life expectancy. Medical and health experts agree that one of the biggest dangers to retired folks' health is inactivity. Many medical researchers, cardiologists and scientists are coming to the conclusion that exercise is *the* key factor in health and long life. Exercise, they believe, is far more important than diet.

Unquestionably, people living in warm climates tend to spend more time outdoors. They can engage in exercise and healthful activities instead of huddling next to the fireplace with eyes glued to the television set. Bicycling, swimming, tennis, daily walks or strolls by the river do wonders for your health and add valuable years to your life. In mild winter climates these are year-round activities, and most cost you little or nothing to participate. In cold weather climates folks generally get exercise of this nature only sporadically, if at all.

Snowbirds

There are those who will say, "Yes, it would be nice to escape winter, but have you ever tried taking a brisk walk or to play tennis in Florida during July?" They have a point here. Although it is clearly possible to get the exercise out of the way early in the morning or after sundown, many people just cannot stand the muggy humidity of the Southern states and do not want to move to the low humidity Western states.

For some folks, the solution to the climate problem is to become "snowbirds" and have the best of all worlds. Snowbirds are those free spirits who choose to escape winter's anger by flying south for the season. When summer's heat threatens to become oppressive, it's back to a kinder, gentler climate. Snowbirds luxuriate in warm, balmy Phoenix winters and enjoy spring-like summers in Montana. Those who choose RV retirement usually do exactly that. There is an in-depth discussion of this lifestyle later on in this book.

Crime and Retirement

Locating in a crime-free area is an important objective for anyone searching for a retirement home. Unfortunately, as you might guess, there is no such thing as a totally "crime-free" community. There are, however, many "low-crime" areas around the country, and they are relatively simple to locate—particularly if you are rich.

Why rich? Because it turns out that the *lowest* crime rates in North America are found in the most affluent neighborhoods! I discovered this fact while studying the FBI's crime statistics for cities with populations over 10,000 in the United States. Until then, I had always assumed that most burglaries and robberies would naturally take place in the wealthiest neighborhoods. Not so; the *richest* neighborhoods generally have exceptionally *low* rates of burglary, larceny and robbery.

None of the foregoing will be of comfort to those of us who are looking for economical yet safe retirement neighborhoods. However, there are many, many low-cost places to retire that are just as safe as the expensive spreads such as Palos Verdes or Westchester County. Read on, and we'll explain how to find them.

There's no question that United States is plagued with crime and violence. We're suffering in a way that we didn't dream of back in the 1930s, when the country was in a depression, when unemployment was 20 percent and soup lines were common sights. Yet if you recall, many folks never bothered to lock their doors at night, and we kids played outside until long after dark. Crime rates were at a fraction of today's statistics.

What's the answer? Some say we need to get tougher on criminals. But how do we do this? We have the highest percentage of our population locked up of any other civilized nation in the world. We cannot build prisons fast enough; prisoners are being kicked out of jail before their terms are up in order to make room for more criminals!

Why Some Places Are Safer

The number of police do not determine low-crime areas. Some large cities have so many cops patrolling the streets they get in each others' way. Nevertheless, the high crime rates there are bizarre. On the other hand, some communities only have part-time police protection, yet burglars are as scarce as honest lawyers. You see, a large police force is usually a *response* to crime not an indication of a town's safety.

As a rule, the larger the city, the higher the crime rate. That should be obvious. Yet, even in large cities, you'll find areas of tranquility, sometimes not too far from the problem areas. When checking out a neighborhood for possible retirement, look for mature, low-turnover neighborhoods where residents know each other, and where the average resident is at or near retirement age. The age of neighborhood residents is important. When a low-cost neighborhood is overrun with young people (particularly males between the ages of 15 and 30), and when most of them are underemployed, you are looking at a troubled neighborhood. The FBI reports that 80 percent of all arrests for property crimes or for violent offenses are males, age 20 years or younger. When seeking a rental or a home to buy, cruise the neighborhood and look for teenagers "hanging out" on the street corners. Try to find a neighborhood with older, mature residents; your chances for peace are better there.

Don't make the mistake of automatically connecting unemployment with crime. Curiously, some parts of the country with high unemployment rates have far less criminal activity than big cities where work is plentiful. Looking for work does not make a person a criminal. The true criminal doesn't *want* to work—that's precisely why he steals.

Drugs and Crime

Why is it that crime rates are so high today when it was low during the depression, when so many were out of work? In those days, young men stood in breadlines rather than steal. Why the difference between today's affluent society and the depression? In a word: *drugs.* In those days, alcohol and tobacco were the drugs of choice—for those who could afford them.

Nothing comes close to drug use as a cause of criminal activity. Some experts estimate that as much as 80 percent of property and violent crimes are drug-related. For the past decade, we have been bombarded with news of a vaunted war against drugs. Twice a year, bureaucrats cynically announce that we are winning the war and that there is light at the end of the tunnel. Yet drugs go on, and crime goes up.

The point to remember is that drug addicts pay for their expensive habits through crime. Burglaries, muggings and robbery are the quickest and easiest way to get money. Therefore, when you live in an area of high drug use, your chances of being burglarized is five times that of living where drugs are not so freely used. Robberies occur 62 times more often in the drug-plagued areas. The solution is to look for places where drugs and crime are not out of control.

One way of doing this, oddly enough, is by studying the local newspapers and seeing how crimes are reported. This can tell a lot about how safe a town is by the importance accorded various crimes. When murder, robberies and burglaries are reported routinely or not at all, you can be sure there is a high level of drug use; when these kinds of crime are covered sensationally, perhaps they aren't so common.

For example: in the summer of 1991, when I was visiting New York City, I noticed a small article in the *New York Times* with a headline that read: "Two Are Shot Dead and Three Are Hurt After a Collision." The killings occurred in Manhattan after a fender-bender at an intersection. Apparently the problem started when someone in the crowd pointed out that one of the cars was blocking traffic. This incensed the driver, so he pulled a gun and opened fire on the crowd of bystanders. Two dead, three wounded. If a horrible thing like this happened in most parts of the world, headlines would have screamed the event on front pages across every newspaper in the country. Yet, in New York City, a crime of this magnitude only rated a one-column story on the corner of page 23—and only then because more than one was murdered. Had it only been one person killed, it probably wouldn't have rated even a one-column headline.

You can't blame the newspaper; murders are so common in that city that if all of them were reported on the front page there wouldn't be room for other news. As a matter of fact, that same article reported that this double murder was just *one of three* incidents that night that involved automobiles and gunfire that ended in death. Don't you find this shocking? Although at least two other humans had been shot to death after traffic accidents that same night, the events were so unremarkable that they only rated a one-sentence announcement on page 23! The victims weren't newsworthy enough to have their names published, so their murders were reported as casually as a stock market report in my home town newspaper.

Therefore, if murders and rapes are reported on page 23, if at all, you can presuppose violent crime to be epidemic. On the other hand, if a burglary makes page one headlines, then burglaries can't be all that common. If a newspaper publishes a detailed police log, read it over carefully. In town where police are mostly involved in cases such as rescuing a cat from Mrs. Smith's tree or recovering a bicycle stolen from Jimmy Jones' front yard, crime probably isn't exactly out of control.

Having said that, I have to point out a contradiction. In *tourist*-oriented communities, a weekly police log can be deceiving. I have a friend who is a police officer in a prime tourist area, and he complains that serious crimes are sometimes not reported in the local newspaper. The police chief and city officials want to present a calm and peaceful front so as not to scare away tourists or potential buyers of resort property. The newspaper reporter is given a list of crimes for the week, but only those the police chief wants to publish. In other words, read between the lines if it's a tourist-oriented area you are considering.

FBI Statistics

For really serious research as to an area's crime status, you can visit your local library and ask for a copy of the latest *FBI Uniform Crime Report*. This publication lists all towns with populations over 10,000 and ranks them as to the various types of crimes. The list is broken down into the types of crime committed: murder, forcible rape, robbery, aggravated assault, burglary, larceny-theft and automobile theft.

Using these statistics, I've prepared the following list of what I consider to be the 100 safest towns and cities in the country. To compile this list, I placed the highest emphasis on crimes such as burglary and the lowest on crimes such as shoplifting. Burglaries have a much greater impact on those trying to get by on a shoestring than shoplifting. As you can see, most of these are smaller towns. But don't hang your hat on statistics; some small towns can be crime ridden and there are very safe neighborhoods in most big cities. Check it out.

The One Hundred Safest Towns and Cities

1 Paducah, Ken.
2 Chapel Hill, N.Car.
3 Greensboro, N.Car.
4 Henderson, N.Car.
5 Ft. Thomas, Ken.
6 Harrison, Ark.
7 Glasgow, Ken.
8 Mill Valley, Calif.
9 Moro Bay, Calif.
10 Murray, Ken.
11 Athens, Tex.
12 Palos Verdes, Calif.
13 San Marino, Calif.
14 Bay St. Louis, Miss.
15 Boone, N.Car.
16 Leesville, La.
17 Edwardsville, Ill.
18 Ashland, Ore.
19 St. George, Utah
20 Arcata, Calif.
21 Franklin, Tenn.
22 Pacific Grove, Calif.
23 Paradise, Calif.
24 Apache Junction, Ariz.
25 Cookeville, Tenn.
26 Lake Havasu, Ariz.
27 Camden, Ark.
28 Tahlequah, Okla.
29 Paso Robles, Calif.
30 Long Beach, Miss.
31 Rogers, Ark.
32 Desert Hot Spr., Calif.
33 Port Angeles, Wash.
34 Henderson, Ken.

35 Los Gatos, Calif.
36 Bend, Ore.
37 Cupertino, Calif.
38 Ormond Beach, Fla.
39 Hanford, Calif.
40 St. Augustine, Fla.
41 Coos Bay, Ore.
42 Grants Pass, Ore.
43 Laguna Beach, Calif.
44 Cocoa Beach, Fla.
45 Fairfield, Ala.
46 Clear Lake, Calif.
47 Bartlesville, Okla.
48 San Luis Obispo, Calif.
49 Roseburg, Ore.
50 Georgetown, S.Car.
51 Ft. Walton Beach, Fla.
52 Aiken, S.Car.
53 Grand Junction, Colo.
54 Forest City, Ark.
55 White Plains, N.Y.
56 Klamath Falls, Ore.
57 Fayetteville, Ark.
58 Monterey, Calif.
59 Kingsport, Tenn.
60 Gainsville, Ga.
61 Cedar City, Utah
62 Yuba City, Calif.
63 Seaside, Calif.
64 Nacogodoches, Tex.
65 Bullhead City, Ariz.
66 Kissimmee, Fla.
67 Carlsbad, N.Mex.
68 Beverly Hills, Calif.

69 Manhattan Beach, Calif.
70 Marysville, Calif.
71 Natchez, Miss.
72 Houma, La.
73 Medford, Ore.
74 Chico, Calif.
75 Bellingham, Wash.
76 Brunswick, Ga.
77 Hilo, Hawaii.
78 Eureka, Calif.
79 Panama City, Fla.
80 Clarksville, Tenn.
81 El Centro, Calif.
82 Vancouver, Wash.
83 Hot Springs, Ark.
84 Porterville, Calif.
85 Boulder, Colo.
86 Santa Cruz, Calif.
87 Harlingen, Tex.
88 Indio, Calif.
89 Muskogee, Okla.
90 Charleston, S.Car.
91 Yuma, Ariz.
92 Rock Hill, S.Car.
93 Redding, Calif.
94 Ogden, Utah
95 Myrtle Beach, S.Car.
96 Cape Coral, Fla.
97 Santa Barbara, Calif.
98 Gulfport, Miss.
99 Asheville, N.Car.
100 Fort Smith, Ark.

Chapter Six

Mobile Home Living

Some folks, when they near retirement, begin thinking of selling their home and "drawing in their horns" by buying a mobile home. Many consider this an ideal way to live in comfort, convenience and on a minimum amount of money. Approximately four million mobile homes in the United States house about eight-and-a-half million people, most of whom are retired. Many parks are exclusively inhabited by retired folks. Those who have chosen the mobile home as a way of life point out that this is one way of home ownership without the high investment and real estate taxes that go with most property. As one couple said, "It costs us only $100 a month to live in our own home. And that includes water, garbage and sewer. We don't pay property tax; we buy a license plate."

Not all mobile home parks are inexpensive, of course; some charge as much as or more than apartment rentals in the same neighborhood. Generally, space rents depend upon the facilities and scarcity of mobile home spaces in the locality. The least expensive space rent we found was a mere $50 a month. (You wouldn't want to live there.) The most expensive mobile home housing we've heard of was a used 1,000-square-foot metal sided home priced at $150,000 with a space rent of $1,180 per month. (You wouldn't want to live there, either—not on a shoestring.)

Mobility

Mobile homes today are anything but mobile. Most are so wide and so long that only specialized companies attempt to move or install them. The manufacturers are trying to change the term to "manufactured" homes, yet the buyers insist on the term

77

"mobile." Curiously, many people still refer to mobile homes as "coaches," a real artifact of early trailer living.

Once installed on a site—joined together into three- and four-bedroom units complete with everything but a basement swimming pool—they are permanently in place. Then, how did they get the name *mobile*? It started after World War II when they actually *were* mobile—only eight-feet wide and rarely more than 35 feet long. Because of a severe post-war housing shortage, hundreds of thousands of house trailers were built and families used them to travel to job locations and as homes. Construction workers found house trailers indispensable; they were easily towed behind the family car and they could be placed near, or sometimes *on* the job site. Although they were the size of today's recreational vehicles, their purpose was not recreation, but housing.

But many families who lived in these temporary housing units felt embarrassed at the concept of "house trailer." They remembered the pre-war days when depression-bruised families were forced to live in dilapidated house trailers because of economic straits rather than as a temporary convenience. Therefore, house trailers became known as "mobile homes." Woe unto the person who accidentally referred to them as "house trailers!"

For Retirement

Some upscale mobile home parks offer amenities such as Olympic-sized swimming pools, hot tubs, jacuzzis, tennis courts, spacious club houses and just about everything you expect to find in expensive apartments or luxury condos. You don't have to worry about landscaping or maintenance of anything but your own small plot of ground. Sometimes, even individual landscaping chores are taken care of by the park management. And, because mobile home parks are frequently enclosed by fences, with limited outside access, they are unusually safe. Some of the more expensive parks are totally closed, with security guards posted at the entrances around the clock. In any case, because the homes are close together, and because residents know each other far better than in traditional neighborhoods, criminal activities are rather quickly noted.

The standard width of a mobile home today is 12 feet wide with lengths up to 70 feet. Some are 14 feet wide. When two of these units are joined together, forming a "double-wide," you end up with a good-size home. The square footage is often larger than the retiree's original home. If you've ever visited one of the expensively furnished display models at your local mobile home sales lot, you've probably been dazzled at the luxury and spaciousness.

What does it cost to live in a mobile home? That's like asking what it costs to live in a house; it all depends on the cost of the house and the neighborhood. We've seen acceptable park spaces renting for as little as $75 a month, and others for much, much more. For example: we looked at a park near Sarasota, Florida that featured a landscaped lakefront, a beautiful clubhouse, tennis courts plus the inevitable swimming pool—for around $215 a month. Used two-bedroom mobile homes were priced at $14,000 to $21,000, with new units starting at $29,000. A social director arranged a full schedule of activities for the park residents. We talked to a retired couple who recently purchased a double-wide home in the park. "We sold our place in Michigan for $50,000 clear," said the husband, "and we considered putting the money into a condo in Sarasota. It was nice—a clubhouse, swimming pool and bike paths. But the monthly maintenance fee was almost what we pay for rent here." His wife added, "So we bought this place for $18,000. It has everything the condo had, and now we have over $30,000 to invest for living income."

Another park, just a few miles away, was full of older units, many 10 to 20 years old, more closely spaced. The major facility was the laundry room—which traditionally serves each park as a major place to meet, socialize and exchange gossip. According to residents, all of whom were retired, there was a satisfactory level of social activity, organized by residents on an informal basis rather than by the park management. It was quite pleasant and peaceful, with mature trees for shade. A few homes displayed "for sale" signs, including a single-wide, one-bedroom place for under $8,000. Park rent was $155 a month. Space rent farther out in the country was even less expensive, as low as $80 a month, according to some park managers. Yes, that's in Florida.

It's interesting to note that many parks—particularly the higher-quality ones—prohibit posting "for sale" signs on the homes. Thus, you might drive through a park and gather the impression that there is nothing for sale. When you cannot find signs, you simply inquire at the park manager's office. Partly this rule is to keep things uncluttered by signs and advertisements, but part of it is management's desire to filter out undesirable tenants they do not want to buy into the park.

Purchase Prices

Prices vary widely, depending on the newness of the mobile home, the condition of the park, but most of all, the scarcity of park spaces in the area. Bear in mind, you are paying for the location rather than the actual value of the home. A mobile home located in a city where spaces are scarce could sell for $30,000 whereas the identical make and year—located in a town where there are plenty of openings—might be worth only $5,000. Mobile home salesmen are quick to claim that this difference in value is appreciation. Appreciation has nothing to do with it; the extra money simply reflects the scarcity of park spaces. When land is valuable, fewer entrepreneurs are willing to devote it to mobile home parks unless there is a good return on the investment. That's why in smaller towns, where land is cheaper, mobile home prices and park rents are far less.

For example: we recently looked at a 14x70, two-bedroom, two-bath mobile, with new appliances, washer and dryer, with a 10x12 storage shed—situated on a large fenced lot for $7,800. In a similar park in a large city the unit would sell for closer to $40,000. Another home, this one an older 10x55 with an expanded living room, also two bedroom, but just one bath, was listed at $3,500, but the owner hinted he would take much less on a cash sale. Had this been in a nice park and in a tighter rental market, it would probably sell for at least $15,000. Remember, the difference in selling price is due to scarcity of land, and not the value of the mobile home.

Pitfalls for Mobile Home Buyers

It's true: a mobile home can be an excellent way of cutting back on living costs. On the other hand, if you're not careful, it could turn out to be a seriously costly and risky investment. Some hazards lurk out there to trip up unwary buyers. A few missteps, and mobile home living becomes far more expensive than owning a conventional home. Some problems can be avoided if you can keep from being blinded by the beautiful furnishings or a dealer's glowing sales pitch. That's only part of it; other important conditions need close investigation.

For one thing, I personally would never purchase a new unit and have it set up in a park. It makes much more sense to buy one already in place, with all the costs known—landscaping, carport, storage shed, and so forth—all in place and ready to use. If the unit is used, so much the better because, despite what a salesman might tell you, mobile homes do *not* appreciate in price like ordinary real estate does. They *depreciate.* The older the unit, the less you should consider paying. Let's examine why.

Although you own your mobile home, the land it's sitting on belongs to someone else. Obviously, you are simply renting a patch of land, from month to month. A problem arises when the park is in an area of rapid development. You could suddenly find that the owner of the property wants to kick everybody off and sell the land for a shopping mall or an industrial park. The land has become too valuable to be kept as a mobile home park investment. This happen all too frequently. When a developer offers big bucks, the park owner can easily succumb to temptation to become wealthy in a hurry instead of counting on your monthly rent.

A situation like this is much more serious than simply the annoyance of having to move your home to another location. Moving one of these so-called "mobile" homes is not a job to be taken lightly. You are at the mercy of professionals who may take full advantage of your plight. That's bad enough, but when all mobile home parks in the area are full, and there is no place to move, your home becomes all but worthless. There is no room at the inn. Even when spaces are available, many parks refuse to accept any unit that is over five years old. The better parks only accept brand-new mobile homes. Worse yet, some parks only accept homes they sell themselves. An out-of-town dealer might offer you a pittance for your unit; he will haul it to some other part of the state where park spaces are abundant.

Scope out the mobile home park situation in the area thoroughly before making any decisions. Talk to park residents where you are thinking of buying. Go to the laundry room and start asking questions. This is easy to do, because the laundry room is not only the nerve center of a mobile home park, but a place where folks are unusually friendly and talkative. While waiting for their clothes to dry, they happily talk each other's ears to stubs. If you ask about the park's management or the owner, be prepared to hear all the good and bad things about living there. Ask residents if they have worries about the park's future. While you're at it, inquire about management's personality. Too often park managers, lowly paid and spiteful, find a sense of power in their new jobs and can become virtual Napoleons. I know of one instance when a new manager forced everyone to get rid of all landscaping shrubs alongside their mobile homes by treating the soil with something like Agent Orange and covering the sterile ground with decorative white rock. "If you don't like it, you can just move," he warned. The next manager decreed that the white rock had to go and grass and shrubs be replanted in the now-dead soil—or else. You don't need a situation where tenants are continually skirmishing with management. An aware and caring park ownership rarely hires this kind of employee.

Check the local classifieds and see if mobile home spaces are listed in the "for rent" columns. If they are, you can assume that park openings are plentiful. Look at the "mobile homes for sale" columns to check prices and visit the parks to see where you might move if you have to. Do this even if you are buying a new unit. You never know.

Another consideration is that a scarcity of mobile home spaces usually cause space rents to escalate far beyond the rate of inflation. My wife and I lived in a mobile home park in San Jose, California for several years. When we moved in, our space rent was a delightfully low $95 a month. Seven years later, when we moved out, the rent was $395! However, that was not the reason we sold our mobile home; it was because of the dreaded "15-year rule."

The 15-year Rule

This is the biggest zinger of all. Many mobile home parks around the nation try to maintain a spiffy image by continually upgrading the homes in their developments. Replacing older units with glitzy new models keeps the park looking new, thus justifying higher rental costs. Managers seldom go around evicting older units, but when possible, they invoke a "15-year-rule." That is, when a mobile home more than 15 years old is sold, it must be removed from the park. If spaces are at a premium in the area, the mobile home becomes practically unmarketable. Most buyers of used mobile homes want a place to *live in*, not a mobile home which they have to *move*. In this type of situation, your depreciation accelerates rapidly and your investment fades quickly as your unit approaches the magic 15-year limit. Some parks have a 20-year limit, but the end results are the same.

Therefore, it's essential to know management's policy on older homes, particularly if you are thinking about saving money and purchasing one that is 13 or 14 years old. Some states and cities have laws prohibiting this age discrimination (Florida for one). A mobile home there can only be evicted for unsafe or unsightly conditions. That's not to say that some park managers won't look for ways to get rid of older mobile homes one way or another. Folks in the laundry room will tell you about this. If a mobile home unit is kept in good condition, one 15 or 20 years old can be an excellent buy, provided it isn't in danger of eviction.

A final caution is against moving into a "family" park—particularly one of the older, run-down parks. Young, low-income families who live in these parks (often on welfare) will crowd into a small trailer with three or four youngsters. Keeping the kids outside, playing in *your* yard, is the only way the parents get any peace and quiet. Too often they exert no control nor show any serious concern over their offspring's behavior. When you have a gaggle of kids trooping through a park in search of entertainment, you not only have noise but you are bound to have vandalism, even if accidental. Youngsters cease to be cute when they start unplugging your electricity, drawing pictures on your automobile or picking your flowers to take home to mommy. (All of these happened to friends of mine who lived in family mobile home parks.) Adult parks are customarily quiet and the chances are that you and your neighbors have something in common.

Having said all of these negative things about mobile home buying, let me say that of all the retired folks we've interviewed, some of the happiest are those living in this lifestyle. It's economical and practically worry-free, as long as you make sure that's the way it's going to turn out. Keep your eyes open and heed some of the advice herewith and you'll be okay.

Buying Your Own Lot

Some mobile home developments *sell* lots rather than simply renting them. This is usually a package deal; they sell you a mobile home as well as the land. One park we visited in Texas offered a $38,900 package (including taxes and fees) for a good-size lot and a two-bedroom mobile home with carport, utility room and a screen room. The development had a 24-hour guarded gate, a swimming pool and tennis courts.

When buying into a development, make sure you actually hold title to the land and not just a revocable lease. A good salesman can make a lease sound exactly like an iron-clad deed. Also be aware that even though you own the lot, you will be liable for monthly maintenance and membership fees. These could be as high as rent in a similar-quality park.

Rock-Bottom Mobile Home Living

Many of those older, eight-foot wide trailers that were popular before the wider ones came into vogue are still around and still in livable condition. In their heyday, they were built for full-time living instead of just summer vacations like most travel trailers today. They were solidly built, sometimes of galvanized steel, and extremely well insulated. Instead of small space heaters, they usually have oil or gas furnaces with forced air heat. Because they have small interior space to heat in the winter or to air condition in the summer, utility bills are almost a joke. The ones that survive make excellent, inexpensive living quarters and, if push comes to shove, they can be moved easily. A pickup or an old Cadillac with a good equalizer hitch can zip them away—no problem—with no special permits or "wide load" warnings front and rear required.

Because these survivors are old-fashioned and clumsy-looking, with birch-finished interiors instead of today's plastic and simulated-wood panels, these older units often go for incredibly low prices. You'll not find them in newer mobile home parks because they've long since been kicked out, to "upgrade" the park. Yet, they make very comfortable quarters, and have surprisingly efficient interiors for storage and everyday living. Beds are usually built in, as is the living room furniture, therefore they need no furniture. You need to inspect them carefully for water damage and dry rot, and you must make sure the undercarriage is sturdy (not rusted through). The next step up from the eight-footer is the ten-foot wide mobile home. These are more spacious and often have eight-foot expansion rooms which make the living rooms or bedrooms a spacious 18 feet wide. When both living room and bedroom are expanded, it's called a "double expando." You don't feel as if you are in a trailer when in one of these. They sell for a bit more than the older units, but far less than the newer 12-footers.

An Affordable Winter Home

These older, inexpensive mobiles are ideal for summer homes in the mountains or winter retreats for escaping freezing weather and outrageous utility bills. For example: we looked at one park in Yuma, Arizona that catered exclusively to retired folks who live elsewhere, but enjoy the warm Arizona sunshine for the winter. Almost all units were "8-wides."

Since the landscaping uses natural desert plants, there is virtually no upkeep problem for the winter residents. Residents pay $180 a month rent (including electricity, water and garbage) while they stay in their winter mobile homes, and then $50 a month through the summer months when the place is abandoned except for the park owners. It's a good deal for the park owners, because for half the year they don't have to bother with tenants—and it works out well for the winter residents because they don't have to pull an RV back and forth every season and then pay $50 a month for RV storage back home. Two were for sale, one for about $8,000 and one for $6,000.

The winter visitors start arriving in Arizona about the middle of November. When they have a quorum at the clubhouse, they elect officers for the season, appoint committee members and decide on a calendar of events. The calendar included trips to nearby Mexico, to Las Vegas and to Disneyland in Los Angeles. Dances, potlucks and card games completed the social schedule.

"We can't afford to stay home," one lady said. "In our Wyoming home, we would be spending at least $250 a month to heat our place. And when the north wind blows, nothing will keep the house warm." She was wearing shorts and a halter as she rode a bicycle around the park. Her husband was out playing golf.

We asked what she figured for a budget during the winter months. She replied, "With $180 for rent, about $250 for food, $100 for entertainment and $200 for miscellaneous, we manage everything on my husband's Social Security check."

Try Before You Buy?

Ordinarily, I'd advise you to rent before deciding to buy. However, for mobile homes, this usually turns out to be impractical. That's because all but the most humble (sometimes sleazy) parks strictly prohibit residents from renting out their mobile homes. This is an almost universal rule: no rentals. Places where renting is permitted are generally places you wouldn't want to live, anyway. This isn't always true, of course, but don't count on finding anything you might like.

We have found one type of exception to the no-rental policy. It's an interesting concept in mobile home living—one we've seen in a few Florida parks, and may possibly be available elsewhere. It's called a "try before you buy" plan. A park near the town of Hudson, Florida is an example of this. Average-looking, well-kept and nicely landscaped—but without a golf course or lake—this park has a limited number of two-bedroom, furnished mobile homes for lease. The minimum stay is three months, the maximum six months. The manager of the park told us, "We don't make money on these leases, but after folks spend a month or two here, getting acquainted, they usually buy. This is our best sales producer."

The manager pointed out that this is an excellent way to discover three things about yourself. First, you will find out whether or not you like Florida well enough to retire there. Second, you will learn whether you like that particular part of Florida. And third, you will discover whether you like mobile home living well enough to retire in one. The monthly charges are stiff, starting at $500 a month, but it includes linens, dishes and cooking utensils, unlimited use of the clubhouse and pool plus lawn maintenance.

Instant Housing

For inexpensive, quick housing on your own land, you can't beat a mobile home. All it takes is someone to move it onto your lot and you have plumbing, electricity and a comfortable place to live. By the way, the best way to buy a mobile home for your property is to look for one of those distress sales mentioned earlier, one of the 15-year-rule disasters which must be moved at any price. When a mobile must be moved, you can cut the asking price drastically.

You will, of course, check local regulations *very* carefully before placing a mobile on your lot. Many localities absolutely prohibit them on private land. In addition, there are several other things you need to investigate, particularly if you plan on buying property out in the country. The following items must be considered.

1. Are electricity and telephone services available? If you have to pay to install telephone and power poles several miles to your place, you might end up paying more for that than the cost of the land and mobile home combined.

2. A good water supply is essential; if city water isn't connected to the property, you'll need to know how much it will cost to bring it in. The alternative is a well, which could be expensive, depending upon the locality. Even if a well is possible, you need to be assured that the water is drinkable. I have a friend who spent several thousand dollars drilling a well through layers of hard rock, only to find the water tastes like sulfur and smells like rotten eggs. Makes for unpleasant showers, to say the least.

3. If city sewer hookup isn't in the picture, likely you'll need a permit for a septic system. Sometimes this is impossible to obtain. Percolation tests may be required, and if your property can't qualify, you could end up using the bathroom at the nearest filling station. If your luck is *really* bad, it will be a pay toilet, so keep a plentiful supply of coins on hand.

4. If your land is truly out in the country, you must be sure you have access easements across other people's property to reach your land. This is not only important for a road or driveway, but for stringing power and telephone lines as well. If your neighbors are not the friendly type, the only way to reach your property could be by parachute.

5. Check your deed for timber and mineral rights. Usually these aren't important, but if your land is in a mining or timber-harvesting area—as in parts of the Ozarks—you could find bulldozers strip-mining your front yard or chain saws rearranging the landscaping.

Buying a Mobile Home *and* Land

The total investment in a mobile home on private land can be quite minimal, but it does entail a bit of work to get set up. Sometimes the obstacles are much more formidable than meet the eye. Frankly, I believe it's better to let someone else do the work; I'd prefer to buy something already set up and ready for occupancy.

During our research travels, we found exceptional buys in mobile homes on their own lots. For example: How does $10,000 sound for a double-wide, two-bedroom unit sitting on ten acres of wooded lands? Or a single-wide on a riverside lot for $9,000? These are common prices to be found in the Ozarks area of Missouri, Arkansas and Oklahoma. One lovely place was a five-minute drive from a boat launching ramp on Lake Tanycomo. The double-wide mobile home was set back among a growth of pine trees, almost hidden from the road, and surrounded by over 10 acres of wooded solitude—with an asking price of $17,000. Of all the landed mobile home setups we've seen the Ozarks offer the best bargains.

It should go without saying that you need to be positive that Ozark living is what you really want. If you crave fishing, hunting, communing with the outdoors—while your spouse cannot stand the sight of dead catfish or stand the thought of doing without HBO on cable TV, it may be time talk about a compromise place to retire.

Chapter Seven

RVs and Retirement

Of all the lifestyles open to low-income retirees, few come close to recreational vehicle retirement for economy. This presumes, of course, that your rig is paid for or that you aren't facing stiff monthly payments.

If you've ever owned an RV, chances are you've fantasized how it might be to actually *live* in your rig instead of merely vacationing. You imagine yourself taking off, and never landing! Following the seasons, catering to your whims, happy as a seagull soaring in the breeze. It's an exciting, awesome idea. You totally change your old lifestyle, rent out the house, put things in storage and set out with no particular destination in mind! The best part is, for those searching for low-cost retirement, RV living can fill the bill. It depends on how you go about it, of course.

This enthusiasm over RV living is comparatively new. Years ago, before the phenomenal growth of the recreational vehicle industry, RVs were primarily used for weekends and summer vacations. Travel trailers were rarely self-contained (although some models had flush toilets which needed to be hooked to sewer connections before they could be used). Pickup trucks with cab-over campers were the forerunners of today's luxury motorhomes. Those few folks who traveled full time in cramped little trailers were considered to be gypsies, eccentrics or adventurers. Living in the back of a pickup was the sign of a loser.

Times have changed and RVs have changed along with the times. Today, uncounted thousands of retired folks spend months at a time in fifth-wheels, motorhomes and deluxe cab-overs. If you still believe RVs are for gypsies, a visit to your local RV sales lot will leave you slack-jawed in astonishment. Instead of the old porta-potty facilities of yesteryear, we find complete baths, including sunken tubs, showers and designer vinyls. Microwaves and deep-freezers are all but standard, as are three-way refrigerators which operate on either propane, the rig's 12-volt battery system or 110-volt park current. Furnishings are lush and tastefully matched to the rest of the decor. Ingenious use of space provides incredible storage room. Therefore, it isn't surprising that many folks spend a lot of time in their RVs during retirement when they finally have time to enjoy them to the fullest.

For most who eventually retire in their RV—either part time or full time—the travel trailer or motorhome starts off as an extended vacation machine. Once a couple or a single discovers how comfortable and light-hearted living can be in an RV, the notion of full-time living cannot be far away. With a motorhome, trailer or camper as your floating homestead, you can afford to tour the country by the seasons, visiting places you've only read about, making new friends at each twist of the road.

Winter Retirement

Trailers, campers and motorhomes by the hundreds of thousands flock toward winter retirement places in Texas, Florida, California and Arizona every winter. This is an ideal compromise for those who refuse to give up their paid-for homes, or who cannot stand the thought of leaving their grandchildren permanently. For winter's duration, they golf, bicycle, stroll the beaches—whatever suits their fancy—instead of huddling inside next to the fireplace. If they feel like fishing, they needn't chop a hole in the ice first. Money saved on heating bills back home pays for a large part of the trip.

Other retirees, particularly those with homes near housing-hungry colleges or universities, make arrangements with faculty or students to rent their places while they travel. Apartment dwellers give notice in time for their November departure, and make application for another apartment for their return in March.

Friendly Neighbors.

By nature, RV travelers are friendly folks. They *have* to be to enjoy parking shoulder-to-shoulder with their neighbors. You'll find few strangers in RV parks. Winter travelers generally have two sets of friends: those who live in their home town and those who live in the RV winter neighborhood. As winter parks begin receiving visitors, old friends meet and celebrate a joyous renewal of last year's companionship. "We've been coming here for the last six years," one lady told us, "and we have more friends in this park than we've ever made back home!"

Another bonus of winter RV travel is that you can be very selective about climate and/or geographical location. When you become bored with the scenery or with your neighbors, or when the fishing gets slow, you simply start your engine and roll on to greener pastures. Or perhaps, roll on to better fishing instead of greener pastures. (Of course, if you insist upon traveling with your pet goat, greener pastures would be nice.)

All part-timers don't travel seasonally; some use their rigs to visit friends and relatives scattered around the country. Since weather isn't the most important consideration, they travel during the uncrowded and inexpensive times of the year. One couple we interviewed has two sons living on the West Coast, a son in New Jersey and a daughter in Miami. "We make it a point to spend a month each year visiting," explained June, a petite brunette who helps drive the 30-foot motor home. "We never wear out our welcome, and we have our own home. We don't have to interfere with our children's privacy by staying in their homes."

RV Parks Galore

RV destinations offer accommodations that vary in quality from super deluxe to extra grungy. Prices vary from costly to free. Later on, you'll find out how you even get *paid* to park! Higher-quality parks generally have certain features in common besides higher prices: swimming pools, Jacuzzis and shuffleboard courts, sometimes even golf courses.

An all-important part of better RV parks is a clubhouse. It's more than just a place to go for a cup of coffee and to meet other RV enthusiasts. The park clubhouse serves as the headquarters for the park's social activities. Dancing, bingo, arts and crafts, jazzercise, card parties, pot lucks and group tours are just a few of the organized pastimes available in the typical club house. There's no excuse for ever being bored.

Space rentals in regular parks vary from as low as $50 a month to well over $300. For example, the most expensive park in Tucson, Arizona (a place called Rincon Country West) charges $355 a month (plus electricity) for the winter months, but only $1,545 for year-round rent. That figures out to less than $130 a month. About half of the spaces are rented out for the year, with the owners leaving their rigs parked there during the summer. The park supplies a full-time social director for the season, with a complete calendar replete with tennis tournaments, swimming, hobbies and just about anything one might wish to do. "Our people don't just sit around twiddling their thumbs," says the park manager, "We don't give them the chance to be bored."

The foregoing is an example of the most expensive. From there on down the prices decrease, depending on the quality and location. Many perfectly adequate RV parks charge as little as $150 a month. One lady remarked, "Our park rent here costs us less than our oil bill if we stay home all winter, so I figure we're staying here for free. We just weatherproof our house and forget it until the snow melts!"

Recently I read an ad in *Trailer Life* for an RV park in Mesa, Arizona. It advertised rates at $7 a day ($49 a week) and boasted a host of attractions. I'll list them here so you can see what you get for $49 a week: clubhouse, ballroom, lounge, library, pool/billiards, card parlor, Olympic pool/jacuzzi, kitchen/snack bar, four tennis courts, putting green, golf driving cage, shuffleboard and horseshoes, exercise gym, lapidary shop, silversmith studio, woodworking shop, ceramics studio, arts and crafts, ping pong, laundry/ironing rooms and sewing room. Apparently the only hobbies they've missed are parachute jumping and underwater basket weaving. (We didn't actually see this park; we're taking the ad at face value.)

Those addicted to slot machines will find many of Nevada's casinos very accommodating for RV travelers. For example, Sam's Town RV park in Las Vegas charges $8.88 per night, which includes (besides hookups) a 56-lane bowling alley, 2,000 slot machines, two floors of casino with keno and a race-and-sports book. As if that isn't enough, they offer free dance lessons. Most casinos don't bother charging for parking; they simply request that RVs park in a designated area, but provide no hookups. By the way, some of Nevada's gambling casinos, starting with Harold's

Club in Reno, have made it a policy to hire senior citizens as part-time or full-time workers. How would you feel about dealing a few hands of blackjack next winter?

There are so many RV parks that we can't begin to describe the various types. Those with their own golf courses present a country club atmosphere, complete with 19th-hole cocktail lounges and gourmet dining rooms. Others sit right on the beach for easy access to surf-casting and splashing around in your bathing suits. There are even parks for nudists, where people splash around in their *birthday* suits! That's right, scattered about the U.S. and Canada are at least a hundred clothing-optional RV parks, where you can swim, play tennis or ride bikes—in the buff if you so choose. Ordinarily, you must be a member of American Sunbathing Association to enter (see appendix for address) but most parks allow trial visits by respectable-looking couples. Monthly RV space rents are usually quite reasonable—$185 a month at one deluxe naturist park in Florida, including full use of facilities, electricity, water and garbage. Since park residents do laundry less frequently, they also save on laundry detergent.

North for a Cool Summer

Seasonal travel is not the snowbirds' exclusive kingdom. Summer heat and humidity send thousands on the reverse trek. Retirees who select Phoenix or Tucson for retirement because of the lovely winter weather can be bored silly by endless, 100-degree plus July and August days. That's why you'll see Arizona license plates in Montana, Michigan and Maine during the summer. Spring and fall are beautiful in Missouri and Indiana, but summers are suffocating and could better be spent elsewhere.

We interviewed one Phoenix couple who regularly visits the Oregon coast each summer. Their favorite town, Brookings, seldom sees summer highs above 70 degrees and the couple always sleeps under an electric blanket. "We've never used the motorhome's air conditioner in Brookings," the husband said, adding, "We've never seen the temperature reach 80 degrees!" Other RVs visit here in the winter, as well, since fishing is good all year and it never freezes. Be prepared for rain, however.

Folks who choose to retire on the gulf coast of Florida because of mild winters dearly love to escape the hot summers there. The hills of West Virginia, North Carolina, Kentucky and Tennessee offer welcome deliverance from Florida's steamy summers. The Atlantic coast, particularly up around Maine, offers some delightfully cool places to park and relax. This might be the time to visit those Canadian RV friends you see every year in your winter neighborhood.

Although RVs are fine for escaping winter cold or summer heat, they are seldom practical for bitterly cold weather. Northern states like North Dakota, Idaho or Vermont—any place where below-zero temperatures are the winter rule rather than exception—are too frigid for all but a few RVs; they're mostly designed for sunny climes. Scanty insulation in the walls and nothing beneath the floors will invalidate all your propane heater's most heroic efforts. Furthermore, RV plumbing is flimsy at best and freezes solid at the first hint of a cold snap.

Of course, a few of the more expensive units are especially designed for full-time living, including winters. They are better-insulated; some are even heated with fuel oil furnaces, rather than inefficient propane or catalyst heaters. They also have electrically-heated water pipes to keep them from bursting. But you'll have to love cold weather to enjoy RVs in sub-freezing weather. Most folks head south for the winter.

Desert Boondocking

The southwestern desert areas draw hundreds of thousands of RVs, the vast majority driven by retired people, as they visit the cities and desert outback for winter stays. They've become a major economic boon for host communities. Yuma, Arizona, for example, doubles its 50,000 population every winter. Phoenix hosts around 200,000 seasonal residents, bringing almost $200 million to the economy. A large number of these visitors bring RVs with them.

The Southwest offers plenty of conventional RV resorts with the usual recreation facilities. They vary in size from 500-space parks to small places with room for just a few RV spaces. But for many, the Desert Southwest presents unique opportunities for *boondocking*: ingenious techniques of camping without paying overnight fees. *Freebies* is another expression for the same thing.

Most every RV owner boondocks occasionally; that's one of their rig's advantages. Roadside rest areas are perfect for getting sleepy RV drivers off the Interstates. A supermarket parking lot can be a lifesaver when it's too late to find an RV park. A friend or relative's driveway is much better for a weekend visit than a motel or trailer park a dozen miles away. Boondocking is convenient—and the price is right.

Southwestern desert boondockers have raised the concept of boondocking to a fine art. They take great satisfaction in crisscrossing the country without ever paying an overnight parking fee. A badge of pride is the ability to spend the entire winter boondocking—enjoying sunshine, companionship and recreation—without spending a nickel for rent. Needless to say, free rent and no utilities helps enormously toward the notion of shoestring retirement. It eliminates the two most expensive items in most budgets.

Desert boondocking started informally many years ago, when a few campers and trailers began pulling off the road onto government land and spending a few days or weeks of just loafing. They'd simply set up camp wherever they pleased and make themselves at home midst the cactus and sagebrush. Because the vast majority of Arizona and California desert lands are public property, nobody complained.

Before long, the word got out that free camping in the desert was the way to spend the winter. Thousands joined the pioneers, then tens of thousands. Every winter, small cities of campers began blossoming all over the desert. The Bureau of Land Management (BLM) didn't know what to do about this. Even though government lands belong to the public, the public doesn't necessarily have the right to "squat" on public lands and spend the winter.

Rather than attempt to evict thousands of RVs, the BLM began selling camping permits for the entire season and encouraging the boondockers to congregate in certain locations. The fee is a mere $25 a year, which goes toward providing drinking water, dumping stations and cleaning up after the campers leave for the summer. Recently, the BLM started offering free campsites (presumably with utilities) for volunteers who will do a small amount of work, monitoring the permit-holding campers and checking sanitary conditions.

Who Are the Boondockers?

Don't get the wrong impression and equate boondocking with poverty. You'll see rigs boondocked in the desert that cost more than many fancy homes. Their owners can afford to spend the winter anywhere they care to, yet here they are, happy campers in the cactus. They come from all walks of life, all trades, professions and occupations. Their politics and religions run the full spectrum as do their tastes in music and literature.

Almost all desert boondockers are retired, and have one thing in common: a love for desert winter retirement. To be sure, there are those who really couldn't afford a winter vacation any other way. In fact some *have* to live this way because their incomes are so low. Therefore, you'll find shabby old homemade trailers and rustic campers on old pickups parked next to shiny new motorhomes and spiffy fifth-wheel trailers. There is an interesting mixture of palatial and mundane, well-off and just-getting-by folks living side-by-side. RV camping is truly a social leveler. This is democracy at grass-roots level (or is it cactus-roots level?).

In addition to the low rent of $25 for the season, boondockers enjoy the lowest utility bills imaginable. They pay nothing, since there are no 110 current plugs in the desert, no water hookups, no natural gas and no garbage/sewer charges. Bottled gas cooks meals and sometimes provides lights. Radios, TV and indoor lights are powered by 12-volt batteries, which are charged by solar panels. Conserving drinking water and battery power becomes second nature after a while. This is living at its simplest—and at its cheapest!

Those who prefer solitude, simply wheel off the road wherever they choose—within the permit area, of course—and drive until all traces of civilization are out of sight. They set up camp and sometimes stay for weeks before having to make a run into the nearest town for supplies. They are disturbed by no sounds other than the distant yapping of coyotes or feisty little birds chattering away in the sagebrush. My understanding is that there are ten BLM campgrounds in Arizona and eight in eastern California, near the Colorado River. Some have improvements such as water and dumping stations, others very little. One, near Holtsville, CA is even said to have a hot tub!

Quartzite: RV City!

Most folks can't stand solitude for very long. They feel a need to be around other people. Now, you might imagine that desert RV camping would be isolation personified. Oddly enough, desert camping can be perfect for the gregarious, the talkative and those who love to make friends, as well as for hermits. This is because every winter, the biggest RV boondocking area of all—Quartzite, Arizona—changes from empty desert into a virtual city. Although rigs don't park cheek-to-jowl, as they must in commercial RV parks, the campers have to get close together to make room for the others. Because so many friendly neighbors are camped nearby, folks who normally wouldn't dream of boondocking feel absolutely secure here.

The Quick-Change Artist

Some claim a million people converge upon the Quartzite boondocking paradise every winter. That's entirely possible, because when you drive toward Quartzite's center, RVs fill the desert as far as the eye can see. Other estimates (probably more accurate), peg the yearly roundup at 200,000. No one knows for sure, since rigs are continually arriving and departing or moving from one boondocking site to another. Whatever the population—200,000 or more—Quartzite becomes quite a city. Then, when the late spring sun begins beating down on aluminum roofs, when air conditioning begins to sound nice, the rigs abandon their city to the baking heat of the summer's desert. They head for someplace where they can plug in the air conditioner.

Throughout late spring, summer and early fall, Quartzite lives the life of a typical desert crossroads community. But when winter rolls around, things change quickly. Entrepreneurs of all descriptions set up shop, selling wares and services to the flood of RV owners who begin arriving in mid-fall. This is where hobbies become businesses and pre-retirement skills once again become valuable as retirees return to the marketplace to ply their trades and engage in their own, pre-retirement specialties. Signs on the front of motorhomes, campers and trailers announce: ALTERATIONS AND TAILORING, AIR CONDITIONERS SERVICED, CERAMICS, AUTO REPAIR, RENTAL LIBRARY. One motorhome advertised:

COPY MACHINE AND WORD PROCESSING, (presumably the rig had its own generator).

People set up stands in front of their rigs to sell knicknacks, clothing, arts and crafts, trinkets and essentials. Computer repairmen and knife-sharpeners compete with booksellers and clock repairmen. Automobile mechanics carry tools in their pickups and bring the garage to your vehicle while they make repairs. One man, who deals in flea-market kinds of merchandise, said, "Whenever my wife and I spend the winter here, we always take home more money than we left with."

The crossroads is embraced by a carnival mood that lasts until the first hot days of spring begin to dull the excitement. Making friends, going to potlucks, dances and club meetings keep the social types busy, and trading paperbacks, conversations over campfires and card games are for the quieter types. An outdoor ballroom called the *Stardusty* hosts more than 200 ballroom dancers at twice-a-week dances.

Unique Slab City

During World War II, General Patton searched for a desert training ground to prepare his armored division for war. He wanted terrain that simulated North Africa's desert, a place to get his tank crews in shape for the planned invasion of North African to fight the Nazis. He found it near the small town of Niland, not far from Southern California's Salton Sea. A large camp went up, the troops readied for battle. After the war was won, the camp was dismantled and abandoned to the low desert. The military is gone, buildings razed to the ground, but the cement slabs upon which the buildings rested are still there—hence the name *The Slabs*, or *Slab City*.

These cement platforms made wonderful RV pads, so it wasn't long before a few campers began spending winters in the sunshine of the Southern California desert. The altitude is low, very close to sea level, making for winters which are as pleasant and balmy as the summers are hot and insufferable. The news quickly made the rounds of RV boondockers. Slab City became a rival to Quartzite. And, instead of the nominal $25 a year, Slab City is free!

Between 5,000 and 10,000 people congregate here every winter, and are said to feed over $4,000,000 into the economy of Imperial county. By June, all but a handful are gone. RV's of all descriptions and prices pull off the paved road, head into the desert and park haphazardly, sometimes parking next to friends, other times seeking solitude. Compatible RVs cluster together, forming regular neighborhoods, each with a central campfire area surrounded by lawn chairs and chaise lounges.

As an anthropologist and a student of cultures and subcultures, I'm fascinated by the social structure of the Slabs, and the way folks interact with one another. My wife and I visited there with our motorhome on several occasions, and we've always been amazed at the wonderful, pioneering spirit of the campers. This must be how it was back in the covered wagon days, for among all of this chaos there is an admirable sense of community and order. There is a heart-warming, natural sense of respect for neighbors' rights. The more religious campers have started a church, complete with regular services. The church, in a mobile home, doubles as an information center when church services aren't underway.

With no formal rules or regulations, the residents seem to know instinctively just what to do as individuals to make things work. Even though there are no law enforcement officers, there are no lawbreakers. When an occasional troublemaker drifts into Slab City, he or she receives a silent treatment that is followed by determined group action should the offender not catch the hint. Residents say they rarely worry about theft, pointing out that many folks, when going into town for shopping, think nothing of leaving belongings behind to mark their parking spot. Sometimes they'll leave everything behind while they visit Mexico or Las Vegas for several days. There are too many folks around for a thief to feel confident about swiping something without being detected.

A calm sense of security pervades the campground. An unspoken notion of the Golden Rule inspires folks to care for their neighbors. Should a camper not appear outside by 10 o'clock in the morning neighbors will check to see if everything is okay. Several RV units have CB radios, always monitoring channel 9, ready to call Niland (about 2 miles away) for medical emergencies, or the rare occasion when someone needs an ambulance or a sheriff's deputy. At any given time, there are several retired nurses staying there, so medical care isn't as far away as it might seem.

Although the majority of the Slabs' residents are retired, there are a few younger families. As a matter of fact, a county school bus makes a daily stop to pick up the handful of children who live there. Once a month, a government agency out of San Diego arrives with surplus commodities, and for some reason, the Salvation Army drops in two or three times a month to distribute vegetables, canned goods and other foods. Some campers need this help; most don't, even though they welcome the freebies. As one lady said, "When you're living on Social Security, you feel that anything the government hands out is something your taxes have already paid for!"

Few places in the country can retirees live so pleasantly for so little. Many Slabs boondockers report that their major expenditure for the winter, besides groceries from the market in Niland, is propane for cooking. Some have solar power panels on their rigs and collect enough power to operate TV and radios. With no rent or utilities, there is little to spend money on at the Slabs. Several retirees tell us that they not only get by on their Social Security checks—they *save* some of it every month! The Niland post office receives many a check for Slab City residents. The extra money spent in the town doesn't go unnoticed by the town residents who deeply appreciate their winter neighbors.

One couple we met there came from Alaska—seasonal workers—he a construction worker and she employed in a tourist hotel. As soon as their jobs go into hibernation for the winter, they catch a flight to Las Vegas, pick up the motorhome they keep stored there and spend the winter loafing around places like Quartzite, Slab City and Baja California. "We need the rest after a full summer," said Jennifer, "and we do get rest here. If we stayed at home for the winter, we'd never leave our apartment except to shop for food, and we'd never see the sun for more than a couple of frigid hours a day. Here, we are actually getting a suntan!" Walter, her husband, agreed, adding that they were extremely pleased with the low cost of an RV winter retirement. A goodly number of the boondockers' rigs bear Canadian license plates, particularly those from the colder provinces.

Not everyone will be happy at Slab City. My wife and I agree that it's fun for a while and that we thoroughly enjoy the extremely interesting mixture of campers. Yet a long-term visit here could grow tiresome. It's a long journey to the nearest decent library, bookstore or shopping center. Before long, we catch up on our reading, grow tired of playing cards with neighbors and grow weary of eating our own cooking and begin dreaming of Chinese food and pizza with anchovies. For a while, I enjoy not worrying about deadlines or telephones, but the truth is, after a while, I miss them.

Sidewinder and Algodones

No description of Arizona-California RV economics would be complete without mentioning Sidewinder and Algodones. Near Yuma, just off Interstate 8 is Sidewinder RV Park, and a few miles farther is Sleepy Hollow, just across the Mexican border from the sleepy village of Algodones.

The last report I have is that monthly fees are from $60 to $80 at both places. The Sleepy Hollow park also has a band that plays for dances every week. The musicians are regulars who come here every winter. Since you can walk to the border, a good many residents come here to take advantage of the inexpensive dentists in the Mexican town of Algodones. Dental work such as bridges, caps and dentures—excellently crafted—cost a fraction of what you'd pay on this side of the border. Eyeglasses, frames and contact lenses are well-crafted, using identical manufacturers as we get in the states, but at drastic reductions in price.

Medical treatments for everything from cancer to arthritis attract many other visitors. Laetril, and who knows what other medicines, are readily available there, treatments that are illegal on this side of the line. These remedies are banned in the U.S. largely because of the medical profession's insistence that the medications do not work—often just worthless vegetable extracts, they say. That may be correct, but I fail to see why anyone would make such a big deal because a terminally ill patient wants to try one last thing.

The Rio Grande Valley

Another very important destination for RV retirees is in the great state of Texas. RV parks throughout Texas draw travelers from all over the United States and Canada. Although there are undoubtedly some Texas boondocking locations, the emphasis here is on traditional RV parks. The main attraction is that part of Texas bordering Mexico: the Rio Grande Valley, a country famous for grapefruit groves, truck farms, and nowadays, groves of RV parks.

Each winter, trailers, campers and motorhomes of all descriptions converge on the Rio Grande valley and become winter retirement abodes for several hundred thousand temporary retirees. "Winter Texans," they're called. They are welcomed by the local businessmen and residents who acknowledge the tremendous boost retirees give the economy. Orange groves, palm trees and 80-degree afternoons make for pleasant living while winter winds paralyze the countryside back home.

Winter retirement in south Texas isn't a particularly new idea. It started back in the 1930s, when midwestern farmers, their activities shut down by cold weather, would make their way to the warmth and sunshine of the Rio Grande Valley. Pulling old-style house trailers or driving homemade campers these cold-weather refugees began arriving in such numbers that this area gained the nickname of "the poor man's Florida."

When RVs came into their own, and when they lost the connotation of "poor," the Rio Grande Valley came into its own for retirement. The number keeps growing. Ten years ago, about 50,000 snowbirds wintered in the Brownsville-Harlingen-McAllen area, but today there are more than 200,000! A boom in RV park construction tries to accommodate the crush. There are well over 500 parks around here, some with several hundred spaces each. One popular RV retirement destination is Mission, near McAllen. More than 10,000 RVs arrive here every winter, with 100 RV parks making room for them. They almost double the year-round population of Mission. Mission bills itself "The Mecca for Winter Texans."

Park Competition

There is an interesting contrast between the lifestyles of the Desert Boondockers and the Winter Texans. While the desert folks pride themselves on living frugally, organizing unique social groups and creating their own entertainment, the Texas crowd prefers having things done for them. Since RV parks are big business here, they compete for winter residents by offering complete programs of entertainment and activities. Social directors plan pancake breakfasts, ice cream socials, square dances and other events to get people mingling and having a good time. Swimming pools, hobby rooms and classes are common features as well as indoor shuffleboard, tennis, dance halls, libraries, pool rooms, sewing rooms and other special halls for recreation and socializing. Even bare-bones parks usually have a lively rec hall to go with laundry facilities. Park rents here are over $300 a month for the truly ritzy places and down to $200 for the more ordinary— certainly within the range of shoestring retirement.

With such a tremendous influx of people every season, pressure is put on stores, restaurants and service enterprises to keep up with the additional demand for goods and services. This naturally creates a demand for seasonal workers. Many retirees state that they have no problem finding work if they so desire. Many RV parks hire their extra help exclusively from their seasonal residents. Stores and restaurants hire them to help out with the flow of business. Some RVers have "steady" jobs, in that they work for the same employer every year.

McAllen is the largest town in this network of retirement cities with Mission, Harlingen and Brownsville filling out the list. Near the mouth of the Rio Grande is South Padre Island, a long, narrow spit of land that also draws RVs. The southernmost tip is covered by the town of South Padre, but just a few miles north civilization gives way to sand dunes, good fishing and RV boondocking.

We've only discussed a small portion of RV seasonal retirement here. There are excellent parks all along the southern parts of the United States, from Florida to the West Coast that make great places to spend the winter. For summer travel the selection is even wider in the north and into Canada.

Wintering in Mexico

Since Texas and the Desert Southwest wintering places are so close to the Mexican border, it would be surprising if RV owners didn't venture farther south for sun and tourism. Of course they do, and they've discovered some uniquely economical places to spend the winter. You will see RVs and RV caravans in all parts of the republic from the U.S. border to Guatemala. Hundreds of RV parks accommodate trailers, campers and motorhomes of all descriptions. For more details about the RV touring in Mexico, see my book: *RV TRAVEL IN MEXICO*, 1989, (Gateway Books, San Rafael, CA. See Appendix.)

The most popular RV winter retirement areas are found in the Baja California Peninsula and in the mainland state of Sonora. Baja is particularly well liked. This is partly because the Baja Peninsula is so dry that much of it is all but uninhabitable and boondocking is "in." Many wonderful beaches have no hotels or tourist accommodations; they spread empty and desolate along the beautiful Sea of Cortez or the rolling Pacific. Without an RV, no matter how rich you might be, you can only glimpse these sights as you drive past. With your own rolling home, you can enjoy beaches and scenery that those poor millionaires must forego.

Almost totally unimproved, these beaches are ideal for self-contained RVs that need no electricity, water or sewer system. A trip to the nearest town every week or two to replenish the drinking water supply does just fine. Like Slab City and Quartzite, the word about freebies and boondocking leaked out and thousands of RVs started making the winter trek to Baja's sunny winter clime. Like birds flocking together, they cluster along the shores and congregate wherever fishing and scenic attractions beckon.

Not unexpectedly, as more and more "Winter Mexicans" crowd the beaches, natives are beginning to see commercial possibilities and they naturally want their share. Beaches often belong to *ejidos*, or Indian communal lands, under tribal control. Even though all Mexican beaches are open to the public, ejidos can charge for overnight parking. That's why many beaches today are no longer free—although they might as well be because camping charges are so low. Typically, a caretaker makes the rounds every evening and asks for a couple of dollars or so to park overnight—depending on the beach. In return, the caretakers make sure things are tidy and keep their eye out for suspicious characters.

The beach where we've spent the most time is Santispac, just south of Mulegé, about halfway down the Peninsula. Several hundred RVs arrive here every winter, starting in October and staying until the weather begins heating up in April. With their rigs lined up along the beach, campfire pits in front, and sometimes a palm thatch *palapa* built for shade, these Americans and Canadians enjoy a bountiful season of companionship, fishing, swimming and just plain loafing.

The ejido beach caretakers also keep their eyes on trailers and palapas left throughout the summer when Baja sunshine makes Death Valley seem cool. From the reports we get, theft is rarely a problem.

"The same folks tend to come to our special beach every season," explains one lady. "It's like a big homecoming every time another rig pulls in. With campfires every evening, it's like a three-month beach party." Her husband adds, "With rent almost free, it costs us less than $300 a month to spend the winter in Mexico. It could be less, but we like to eat breakfast at the beach restaurant and we often eat dinner in town."

Like Slab City and Quartzite, the "regulars" get to know each other and to expect to see their friends every November through March. Should someone not appear for the season, the others worry about it and might drive to the village to make phone calls to the States and see if something is wrong. Also like Slab City and Quartzite, the residents recognize an unwritten code of conduct that requires respect and courtesy for others. It's truly amazing to see how humans instinctively work together in cooperative and friendly unison. Perhaps it's civilization that causes frowns, impoliteness and selfishness to ruin one's day. Here in Baja, there is none of that foolishness.

Baja RV Parks

For those who hesitate to boondock (although with several hundred rigs in a row, it hardly seems like boondocking), over a hundred RV parks are scattered about Baja. You'll find one just about anywhere anyone would want to visit, as well as places you wouldn't visit on a bet. Facilities range from super-luxurious five-star resorts to rustic fishing camps with no amenities other than cold beer and friendly faces. (What else do I need?)

By the way, 99 percent of your RV neighbors will be from the United States or Canada, because Mexicans almost never own RVs. The ones who can afford them prefer to stay in first-class hotels when traveling. They don't understand why we think traveling in a small tin box is fun. (I don't either, but it *is* fun.)

Space rents for RV parks range from a couple dollars a day to one luxury place that charges $18 to $20 a day. One of our favorite commercial parks is at Bahía de Los Angeles. There, a cement patio and an electrical hookup costs about $4 a day. A water truck passes through with drinking water, and will fill your tanks for about $1.50. The sea provides a bountiful harvest of clams and scallops, not to mention fish for those willing to toss a line in the water. Kids knock on the door every evening to see if you want to buy their freshly-caught fish or live pin scallops, still in the shell. Can't get fresher than that. A nearby restaurant serves excellent meals of fish, lobster and tough but tasty Mexican steaks.

Two little markets in the village supply rudimentary foods such as chickens, coffee, and sterilized milk. Folks on tight budgets depend on the sea for much of their food, with clam chowder, sauteed scallops or rockfish fillets *Veracruzano* providing wonderful gourmet dinners. "We load up our cabinets with canned goods and such before we leave San Diego," said one lady in Bahía de Los Angeles. "We seldom have to buy any groceries here other than fresh eggs and tortillas from the *tienda* and veggies from local gardens. We feel as if we are eating for free." They made a deal with the park's owners for $190 for two month's space rent. "So, I don't see how we could possibly spend any more than $500 out of pocket for two months," said her husband, "and that's including the gas to get here and back!"

Driving and Safety in Mexico

When driving in Baja during our last trip, I counted the number of vehicles on the road and noted that about half of them were RVs with U.S. or Canadian license plates. Sometimes it looked as if we *norteamericanos* had taken over the peninsula for our own campgrounds. My personal experience has been very positive in Mexico after many years of driving cars, jeeps, motorhomes and pulling a vacation trailer. We've handed out questionnaires to RV travelers in Mexico, and one of the questions concerned safety. Unanimously, people said they felt very secure driving in Mexico. Well, that shouldn't be too surprising, because otherwise they wouldn't be there. In any event, if you are interested in visiting Mexico, see Chapter Eleven for more details about driving there.

Also in Chapter Eleven is the adventure of a retired couple who decided to take their RV to Guatemala and study Spanish. This may not be a trip I'd recommend to just anybody, but it does sound as if it would be fun. I'll be reporting further on Guatemala in my forthcoming book *CHOOSE COSTA RICA* (Fall 1992) which will cover retirement in both countries.

Chapter Eight

Full-time RV Retirement

For many adventurous souls, full-time RV living can be the ticket to a new lifestyle and a new world of travel. While some folks really have no choice but full-timing, because it is the only way they can make it on their limited incomes—others choose to full-time because they love the freedom and excitement in travel. This is an excellent way to combine economy of living with adventure.

We talked to a lady who makes her home in a 24-foot motor-home, and she told us: "Last winter, when I left my Michigan home base to go to the California desert, I found I could easily get by on $350 a month." She went on to add that during the winter before she started full-timing, her fuel oil, gas and electric bills at home totaled close to $300 for one month, so getting by on $350 was easy.

Not everybody can manage full-timing on $350 a month, of course. We all know individuals who spend more than that on cigarettes and booze. Well, how did our friend do it? She stayed at Slab City for zero rent where the gentle desert climate all but eliminated the need for heat or air conditioning. Slab City has no utility hookups anyway. She used three five-gallon tanks of propane for cooking and an occasional touch of warmth when the temperature dropped below 60 degrees outdoors. A solar panel supplemented her 12-volt system for lights, radio and cassette player (TV reception is lousy in Slab City). Therefore, her total utility costs came to less than $25 for the full three month sojourn—an average of $8 per month.

"Since I am single, my food costs are low," she said. "Neighbors at Slab City always share rides for shopping in Niland, so I drove the two miles to town just once a week. I needed to dump my holding tanks anyway. My total driving was a little over 50 miles for the entire stay. My gasoline bill was almost nothing."

In addition, she shared expenses with three other single ladies for a day trip to Mexico (about an hour's drive) plus one overnight expedition to challenge the slot machines and blackjack tables in Nevada (about four and a half hours away). "We shared a large room—senior citizen rate of $33 with two double beds—and we took advantage of the 99-cent breakfast specials and the enormous buffets in the casino restaurants. That was the only month that I spent $350, and then only because I couldn't make the slot machines pay off."

Below is an accounting of her winter in the desert. This chart doesn't attempt to count in other fixed overhead for the year, things such as dental bills or home base expenses. The chart simply reports her actual out-of-pocket costs for the three-month vacation in the sun.

RV Sample Budget—$350 Monthly

Budget Expense	3 Months	Monthly
Food	$570.00	$190.00
Campground fees	—	—
Gasoline	$ 8.00	$ 2.70
Propane	$ 21.00	$ 7.00
Laundromat	$ 24.00	$ 8.00
Entertainment (Nevada, Mexico)	$105.00	$ 35.00
Forwarding & postage (daughter)	$ 10.00	$ 3.50
RV insurance (prorated)	$150.00	$ 50.00
Clothing (sweater)	$ 30.00	$ 10.00
Club and organization dues	$ 30.00	$ 10.00
Other expense	$ 31.50	$ 10.50
Totals	$979.50	$326.70

Although these figures do prorate yearly RV insurance and club memberships they do not take into account expenses getting to Slab City. Gasoline and oil changes amounted to $175. By adding these costs to her total auto expenses and prorating over the year, the monthly cost of her vacation was still well under $400.

When we asked Jennie Studdard of LoWs (Loners on Wheels) how RVers managed to get by on so little she said, "Don't eat dinners out, cook everything at home. Buy second-hand clothes, and pinch pennies." She also advised against late model motorhomes. "I want something that uses regular gas and doesn't have all kinds of electronic gadgets. I know lots of good shadetree mechanics who can fix the older rigs, but when it comes to high-tech equipment, we're all lost."

Full-timing on a Budget

To determine how much money it takes to full-time, we sent out several hundred questionnaires. We compared these with an additional 300 queries we sent out the previous year to folks who are retired in conventional housing. We asked RV retirees what they considered to be a minimum outlay for ordinary, everyday living, and also what they supposed an average couple might spend on items like park rent, food, vehicle insurance, and so forth.

The results were somewhat mixed. Some RV people reported they needed as much as $300 a month for groceries while some (singles) claimed they spent as little as $50. In answer to the question: *What would you consider a minimum monthly outlay for your lifestyle?* the replies ranged from $1,500 a month to a low of $325 a month. The surprising thing is the number who couldn't tell us exactly what they spent on any one particular item, because, "I don't keep track of those things." They could, however tell us the total outlay.

The couple who spent the most money per month, figured $1,500 for minimum living costs, which seemed rather high, certainly out of the shoestring class. Then we noticed that under the category *Your Favorite Destination?* the reply was Palm Springs. The lowest monthly estimate was $325, from a single person who listed Slab City as her favorite destination. The majority of the folks answering the questionnaires listed their total costs around $700 a month, with many under $600. Note that none of these figures include depreciation or replacement of the RVs.

RV Food Budgets

The widest range of budget items was for food. Actually, most couples said they spent about $200 a month for groceries and singles around $150. It was interesting to note that those who lived part-time in RVs reported that they spend less for food while in the RV than they do at home. When a few singles reported they spent only $50 a month, we just could not believe this possible. So we called one of our respondents and asked her for a sample menu. She graciously submitted a seven-day menu of which we'll look at just the first three days to give you an idea:

BREAKFAST
SUNDAY: 1 pancake, 2 slices turkey bacon, 3 cups hot tea.
MONDAY: Oatmeal w/raisins, 1 slice toast, 1/2 banana, 3 cups hot tea.
TUESDAY: 2 biscuits & jelly, 3 cups hot tea.
LUNCH & DINNER (often I only eat two meals per day)
SUNDAY: Chicken-rice gumbo, tossed salad, cup choc. pudding, iced tea.
MONDAY: Broiled fish, tossed salad, creamed corn, fresh fruit.
TUESDAY: Noodles w/cheese sauce, sliced tomatoes/cucumber, canned ham, iced tea.
ALTERNATE MENUS
SUNDAY: Leftover chicken-rice gumbo, steamed veggies, pudding cup, iced tea.
MONDAY: Pinto beans, cornbread, coleslaw, fruit yogurt, iced tea.
TUESDAY: Canned salmon, brown rice, cornbread, tossed salad, piece of fruit, iced tea.

She admitted that she snacked in between meals on fresh fruit, nuts and raw veggies, but avoided junk food. After analyzing her diet, we came to the conclusion that she truly has a handle on her food expenditures and enjoys a healthy, as well as tasty and inexpensive, diet.

Other Budgets

The question of how much it costs to live full-time in an RV is a complicated one. All of us have different incomes and budgets within which we must live. Our lifestyles vary as widely as do our budgets. Those with huge mortgages on a deluxe motorhome will naturally spend a lot of their income on payments. Some spend a lot of time driving from place to place, consuming gasoline or diesel fuel and staying in fancy resorts every night. Getting from one place to another isn't cheap since fuel consumption is higher than normal driving. But the average RV full-timer moves only to change locations for the season, and ideally, the rig will be paid for. Renting park space by the month rather than by the night reduces costs drastically. The truly economical lifestyles include a considerable amount of boondocking and freebies.

The following are RV full-timing budgets which were submitted by folks answering our questionnaires. Members of the RV club Loners on Wheels were particularly helpful as they responded to a plea in their club newspaper for assistance. Two of the budgets are for single persons, one a woman, the other a man, both 62 years old. It should be easy to extrapolate for a couple's expenses, since the basics are covered, only additional food costs need be considered.

RV Sample Budget—Rock Bottom Retirement

Budget Expense	Yearly	Monthly
Food	$1,800.00	$ 150.00
Gasoline	$ 204.00	$ 17.00
Propane	$ 102.00	$ 8.50
Clothing and Laundry	$ 180.00	$ 15.00
Entertainment	$ 720.00	$ 60.00
Forwarding and Postage	$ 60.00	$ 5.00
Medical insurance	—————	—————
Vehicle repairs & maint.	$ 420.00	$ 35.00
Vehicle insurance	$ 504.00	$ 42.00
Storage rental	$ 300.00	$ 25.00
Club dues	$ 50.00	$ 4.17
Other expense	$ 496.00	$ 41.33
Totals	**$4,836.00**	**$ 403.01**

This budget was submitted by a single lady who cuts her rental expenditures by volunteering. She recommended the publication by the American Hiking Society, *Helping Out in the Outdoors* (see Appendix) as a source for finding places where you can park free in return for work or acting as a campground hostess. With free hookups, she manages to keep expenses down while enjoying interesting times in wildlife refuges and parks in Texas and Washington state. Other than propane and gasoline for trips into town, she has few extra expenses. She does this for eight months of the year and visits family the rest of the time. Her total income is $1,100 a month, of which she banks $700 (except for months when there is a wedding in the family or other special occasions that call for a splurge). Her medical insurance is covered under her company's retirement plan until she reaches the age of 65, when Medicare will take effect.

RV Sample Budget—Mid-Range Retirement

Budget Expense	Yearly	Monthly
Food	$1,909.00	$ 159.08
Campground Fees	$1,468.00	$ 122.33
Gasoline	$2,236.00	$ 186.33
Propane	$ 190.00	$ 15.83
Clothing and Laundry	$ 508.00	$ 42.33
Entertainment	$ 720.00	$ 60.00
Forwarding and Postage	$ 100.00	$ 8.33
Medical insurance	$ 360.00	$ 30.00
Vehicle repairs & maint.	$ 108.00	$ 9.00
RV insurance	$ 808.00	$ 67.32
Club dues	$ 216.00	$ 18.00
Other expense	$ 200.00	$ 16.66
Totals	$8,823.00	$ 735.23

This is the budget experience of a single man who prefers living in conventional RV parks where he can socialize and perhaps con someone into a game of pool at the clubhouse from time to time. However, the year of this budget saw him boondocking in Baja California for two months and spending a month parked on his daughter's property in Florida, which accounts for rent averaging only $122. He has a fairly new rig, so his maintenance is limited to oil changes and tune-ups (which he does himself). He also has a membership in a nation-wide RV park chain, so he manages to do a certain amount of $1-a-night camping. As a Canadian citizen, he pays $30 a month for the national health care system for full coverage.

RV Sample Budget—Upper-Range Retirement

Budget Expense	Yearly	Monthly
Food	$ 3,300.00	$ 275.00
Campground Fees	$ 3,120.00	$ 260.00
Gasoline	$ 600.00	$ 50.00
Propane	$ 120.00	$ 10.00
Clothing and Laundry	$ 960.00	$ 80.00
Entertainment	$ 1,200.00	$ 100.00
Forwarding and Postage	$ 100.00	$ 8.33
Medical insurance	$ 960.00	$ 80.00
Vehicle repairs & maint.	$ 600.00	$ 50.00
Vehicle insurance	$ 700.00	$ 58.33
Storage rental	$ 420.00	$ 35.00
Club dues	$ 75.00	$ 6.25
Other expense	$ 1,000.00	$ 83.33
Totals	**$12,855.00**	**$1,071.24**

A couple, both 65 years old, submitted this budget. Their total income is over $2,000 a month, but they reported that they only spend half of it. "We don't like to economize on food," the husband said, "and we usually stay at better parks, where there are plenty of things to keep us entertained. That's why we spend more than some others we know." They prefer Florida in the winter and the Northeast, sometimes Canada, for the nicer months. They own a late model motorhome and drive about 15,000 miles a year.

High on the Hog

Of course, RV living can be expensive, depending on how you go about it. We've seen enormous motorhomes, with huge diesel engines, TV cameras scanning the rear, satellite dishes—everything but a full basement rathskeller—selling for over $250,000. That's nice. But folks who can afford one of those, don't need to read this book. If they paid cash for their rig, the combined depreciation and loss of interest income on the money invested would allow a couple to live very well indeed. If they have to make payments and pay interest as well, the outgo would be staggering for most of us.

My point here is to warn folks away from getting starry-eyes and loose checkbooks when looking at RVs. The RV lot sales staff are experts at figuring out how much money you are worth and extracting the maximum. They paint idyllic pictures of your living a super-luxurious life in this motorhome or fifth-wheel-and-truck combo, and they make you feel you cannot possibly live another day without it. (And you'd better hurry, because this special price is for this week only!) Before the buyer understands the process, all of the proceeds from the sale of their home are plunked down on the 35-foot Super-Liner Special with the wetbar, wine cellar and king-size bedroom. And it begins to depreciate the moment signatures appear on the bill of sale. The time to buy one of these luxury rigs is before you retire, when you have income to cover the payments.

Don't let a dealer flimflam you with claims that new rigs are actually cheaper. They'll point out that a new RV can be financed for ten years, thus making payments on the new rig slightly less than that on an older one, which can only be financed for three years. Yes, the payments are lower, but the cost and rate of depreciation are higher! I feel very strongly that if you cannot afford to pay cash, lower your sights to a rig that you can handle comfortably. The time for high payments is *before* you retire, when you have income. There are plenty of folks out there who've grown tired of life on the open road and are willing to sell— cheap—and cash talks. And, for goodness sakes, do not fall in love with the first rig you see.

As far as trailers are concerned, they depreciate rapidly for the first few years, and very slowly after that. There's not as much to wear out as there is on a motorhome. No matter what you decide upon, count the money you invest in a rolling home as non-interest-paying savings, and count the interest it doesn't pay as part of your monthly costs.

Getting Started

Most folks ease their way into full-timing, and this is the advised way to go. Dick March (president of Loners on Wheels) suggested the following stages or levels of RV commitment.

1. Weekenders—have favorite places to visit nearby and who rarely stay more than a couple of days before returning home.

2. Theme-inspired Travelers—follow a hobby, i.e. Blue Grass (or other music festivals), fishing, hunting, genealogy, history, square dancing and the "just-can't-stand-that-ice-and-snow" type.

3. Flea Marketeers—collect junk and treasures, scrounging garage sales and second-hand stores for merchandise to sell or trade at flea markets. They lose money on every sale, but make it up in volume.

4. Two-basers—have one summer base and one winter base, traveling back and forth exclusively between the two bases. Often the home base is their house.

5. High-profilers—ego-driven owners of half-a-million-dollar motorhomes with endless electronics, communications, hot tub, wine cellar and so forth. After spending a fortune on equipment, they delight in boondocking, feeling good about saving money.

6. Chuck-it-all Full-timers—totally succumb to the gypsy call of the road. They usually belong to several RV clubs, such as Good Sam, Escapees and other organizations that cater to full-timers. They keep in touch through club newsletters and correspondence via mail-forwarding services. The longer they are full-time, the wider their network of friends. These are the elite of the RV set.

Some folks jump right into RV full-timing and enjoy that lifestyle for the rest of their lives. But statistics show that most return to conventional living within a few years, or they at least establish a "home base" somewhere. Keep this in mind when preparing for the open road.

What Will the Kids Think?

A big problem for many retirees who want to start full-timing in their RVs, is the shock, disbelief and disapproval of their children. They cannot believe that their parents could do such a thing. The whole idea seems irresponsible to them. "Why do they want to worry us like this? Why do they have to do weird things? Why can't they stay home and be like everyone else?" Yet, they forget about the times *we* worried about the weird clothes they used to wear, the beards, long hair and crazy hippie costumes, or the times we worried about what kind of drugs they were doing at those gawdawful rock concerts.

As one lady put it, "My only real problem getting started into full-timing was convincing my children, relatives and friends that I had not lost all my senses. To them, 'Grandmother' means dressing in a long skirt, apron, bonnet and high-top shoes. She is a person who sits by the fire, knitting sweaters while cookies bake in the oven. 'Grandmother' certainly doesn't mean flitting around the country alone in a little motorhome, dressed in sweatshirt, jeans and sneakers!"

If you want to humor the kids a bit, you can put a CB radio or cellular phone into your rig and get car insurance with a good emergency road service provision. But in the final analysis, it's your retirement and now it's your turn to worry them a little.

One caution that all experienced full-timers will give to new-comers: Don't burn your bridges. You may want to recross them should you decide that full-timing is not as romantic as you thought. If you own a home, you might consider leasing it out for a year or two, "just to make sure." Some make arrangements with their tenants to reserve the garage, perhaps a couple of rooms or the basement for storing their "things." An arrangement is then made with the renters to forward mail and telephone messages.

We've talked to many retirees who started out as full-timers, convinced that they would never again be "tied down" to a house, but who eventually found their dream home and settled down. One couple we interviewed told of selling everything and moving into their fifth-wheel, fully confident that this would be their life for the next decade. But a week later, they stumbled upon a town which they fell in love with. They ended up trading their rig for a mobile home and that was the end of their full-timing experience.

Establishing a "Home Base"

While it might seem that retiring full time in an RV would mean a complete "break" with the present, and a totally free existence, most find this not entirely possible. You will need a home base somewhere.

Even if it's nothing more than a storage shed and a post office box, you need some roots. The mail carrier cannot and will not chase your rig down the highway to deliver Social Security checks, income tax forms or state license tags. You need an address for the grandkids to send birthday cards and graduation announcements. If you plan on using credit cards, you must provide an address. Very handy is a phone number for friends and relatives to pass messages along to you.

There are several strategies for establishing a home base. Some put the burden of forwarding correspondence, paying bills and similar chores on their children. Most kids are happy to do this, since it gives them a feeling of contact with their insane, gypsy parents. Often they will have storage space in the garage or attic for some of those hard-to-part-with items such as those power tools that can't fit in your rig, a 40-year collection of snapshots and 8mm movies or your sewing machine and that 20-ton collection of *National Geographics*. Occasional visits, parking in the kids' driveway, keep the family in contact and give you an opportunity to catch up on your income taxes and other legal duties.

Your home base could also be an inexpensive house, a mobile home or a reserved space in an RV park—any place with storage—and your mail forwarding problems can be turned over to individuals who do this for a living. A look through the various magazines and newsletters devoted to RVing will turn up many such services. Some mail forwarding businesses maintain an 800 number so you can call toll-free to retrieve messages or to leave them. Some services will deposit checks into your bank account and write checks to pay your bills.

Another practical solution is to join one of the RV clubs that cater to full-timers, such as The Escapees. Mail is forwarded, messages recorded and communication problems are resolved. For those buying an RV lot in one of the Escapee "retreats" (landed parks), a storage shed provides secure storage while out on the road and a place to live or park when not traveling.

A home base is good for a few months comfortable rest from time to time. The children finally have a place to come and visit, and you'll have a chance to use those power tools to make repairs on the motor home's roof.

For important mail like IRS forms, full-timers commonly designate an accountant or tax preparer to receive income tax mail. Your children or close friends can also be authorized to accept mail and take appropriate action.

Free Parking in National Parks

Perhaps the main reason you wanted an RV in the first place was to visit scenic national parks, recreational wonderlands and picturesque parts of the country. Making camp alongside a forested lakeside glade or beside a sparkling trout stream—that's what it's all about, right? But, before you retired, you were restricted to your two-week vacation and you had to pay a daily parking fee. That is, providing that you were able to make a reservation on the campsite. Campsites full, it was off to an $18 a night commercial park with hundreds of toad-like children screaming underfoot.

Well, the good news is: if you own your own transportable housing, and if you are retired, the state or federal government will reserve a prime campsite for you at no cost whatsoever! You stay the season for free. Even better, some parks will even *pay* you to park for the entire season! While the pay may be minimal, the work is also minimal, yet interesting and rewarding.

Every vacation season, county, state and national parks are in need of paid and volunteer workers. So are private resorts, campgrounds and tourist attractions. Often, housing units are there for the workers, but space is limited; living accommodations can be provided for only so many people, the rest must be turned away. However, when you bring your own housing with you, it's a different story. They love their RV staff members!

Since many volunteer and paid jobs are in rustic locations, managers and employers are delighted to find seasonal workers who need nothing more than water and electricity hookups. Then, when the season is over, the workers pack up and move on to better weather, leaving behind nothing but good memories. Often before they leave, arrangements are made for the coming season.

Jobs opportunities are: campground managers, bookkeepers, off-season caretakers, maintenance and gate-keepers. The most common volunteer jobs offer free parking and hookups (but no salary) to campground "hosts," whose duties consist of answering questions of new campers and making them feel at home. Other jobs require more responsibility and offer a salary.

One couple called the local county parks department and asked if there were to be any openings for campground hosts at a particularly lovely park where they wanted to stay. "No," came the reply, "We don't use campground hosts." The lady calling asked, "Why not? It won't cost you anything." The head of the department thought that over for a moment, and then decided to give it a try. The couple parked their motorhome by the lake, hooked up to free power and spent the summer simply talking to visitors and answering questions.

We interviewed another couple who spent the summer of 1991 at a county park on a scenic, whitewater river, a favorite place for river rafting and trout fishing. This was their first time doing this. At the end of the summer, they were a bit tired, but enthusiastic. "We sent out ten applications," Brenda said, "and within the week we received two positive replies. We took this one because it paid a monthly stipend as well as the free hookups." Her husband said, "They even installed a telephone in our trailer, so we could be in contact with park headquarters."

The day after Labor Day, their three-month stint completed, they were packing up for their return to their Arizona home base. Asked whether they would do it again, they replied, "Actually, we're thinking about trying for a place in Arizona for the winter. However, next time we'll look for a volunteer job instead of paid, because the campers kept us so busy collecting their overnight fees, we didn't have time to do much fishing."

When asked how much their summer on the river cost them, they did some mental calculations and Joe said, "We were spending about $65 a week at the market. We know, because we only drove into town twice a week. Our only other expenses were laundry, telephone calls to our kids and dinner out once a week." Brenda added, "Video cassettes, too. We rented four or five a week. No television here." After doing some work with a hand calculator, they came up with an average figure of $293 a month. They didn't mention their pay, but it surely covered a portion of their expenses.

RV Work Opportunities

Seasonal jobs with free parking aren't limited to national or state parks and campgrounds—not by any means. When a seasonal migration of snowbirds descend upon a popular RV area, temporary employees are in great demand at the resorts. Handymen, cooks and workers of all types usually receive free rent in addition to salary.

Almost every business in town needs extra help to handle the increased tourist traffic. From gift shops to garages, from restaurants to recycling, temporary help is needed. RV mechanics and repairmen can write their own agendas when thousands of RVs are in town.

Temporary jobs in RV parks and campgrounds can be: assistant managers, clerical staff and groundskeepers. When the RVs pull out, the RV park's staff often drops back to just the manager. Ski instructors are needed in mountain resorts for the winter and fishing guides are needed for the summer. Christmas tree lots love to have commissioned salespeople who can park their rigs in the middle of the trees and watch over them at night. Other salespeople follow trade shows or shopping mall promotions, manning booths and selling items to the public. These traveling jobs would be impractical if you had to stay in hotels and eat in expensive restaurants.

Workamper News

While RV travelers are looking for paid or volunteer jobs, many employers are seeking employees who can supply their own housing for temporary or full-time positions. The *Workamper News* brings everyone together. This publication started a few years ago as an eight-page newsletter to inform RV travelers of both volunteer and salaried jobs available to them. The first issues carried about 35 job announcements. Today *Workamper News* has grown to 24 pages with an average of more than 100 listings representing thousands of openings.

Some jobs listed pay salaries or hourly pay and other benefits while others are volunteer positions with little more than free hookups. Not all help-wanted ads are exclusively for RV owners; some have staff housing available. The publication has been used by a wide variety of public and private enterprises with great success. Since the publishers try to weed out phony get-rich-quick schemes, most help-wanted ads are legitimate. Each listing includes location, duties, benefits, how to apply and who to contact. According to the publisher, there are often more jobs than people to fill them.

Other services of the newsletter are situations wanted ads (first 50 words free) and a resume referral system. Resumes from active job-seekers are maintained on file and are scanned for those which meet the employer's requirements, such as skills, geographic location, benefits and length of employment.

The following jobs were advertised in a recent issue: A Montana dude ranch needed cooks, kitchen help, waiters/waitresses and housekeeping workers. A caravan-tour company wanted wagonmasters. Numerous mobile home parks and RV resorts wanted managers and maintenance personnel. Yosemite National Park wanted roomskeepers, food service workers, sales clerks and other employees. Yellowstone National Park wanted help in sales, grocery, food service, auditing, cooks and other jobs. Many state parks advertised for campground hosts, some with salary. A deluxe, 4-star Florida beach resort offered full hookups in exchange for some grounds maintenance. Each issue lists commission jobs, such as working Christmas tree lots, demonstrating computer software and selling resort lots. The number of job possibilities was impressive.

RV Clubs and Retirement

Many RV travelers feel that part of the fun of owning a rig comes from belonging to a club. Rallies, camp-outs and tours are just a few of the organized activities available through RV Clubs. Newsletters keep members well informed about upcoming events. Depending upon the season and weather, club members meet at designated campgrounds, set up an enclave and begin a time of enjoyable socialization. Bingo, dances and potlucks get everyone together, and they share experiences, advice and recipes. If you're having trouble with your battery system or if your roof leaks, there will always be friends who've been through the same difficulty and who can straighten things out for you. There are clubs for rockhounds and prospectors, for jewelry-making, quilting, handicapped travelers, computer buffs and just about any kind of hobby you can imagine and for which you aren't likely to be arrested. Anything you want to know about RV lifestyles, you will learn by belonging to one or more clubs.

For the full-time RV traveler, however, club membership is more than just an entertaining pastime; membership is essential.

Folks who scrimp by on very limited budgets and who must squeeze the maximum value from every dollar do not hesitate spending money for club dues. They consider club membership every bit as important as gasoline when living full time in their rigs. Typically they belong to more than one club, two at a minimum. One organization is usually the Good Sam Club, which comes with the special RV insurance sold by the club. My understanding is that few insurance companies are thrilled with insuring RVs and few if any offer road service. In addition, most RVers belong to one or more special interest clubs.

For those who want to travel extensively or possibly full time, a full-timer club such as Escapees is a good choice. For those who are single, several RV clubs specialize in services for unmarried travelers. The largest and best known of these single groups is Loners on Wheels. Supportive members, an informative newsletter, club campgrounds and campouts all over the country, make the transition into long-term RVing far more fun. (See Appendix for listing of RV clubs.)

Belonging to clubs takes you out of the realm of being alone. You'll find friends wherever you go. Club publications present news of rallies, of new campgrounds and keep you posted on other members' whereabouts. Some list free parking places provided by members for the overnight use of fellow members. The sticker on your RV announcing that you are a member breaks the ice with an invitation for other members to introduce themselves. Boondocking on BLM lands or in free locations with friends becomes a pleasant, vacation-like experience. You are able to enjoy the inexpensive benefits of RV ownership without feelings of uneasiness about being a stranger among strangers.

Good Sam Club

The largest RV club of all, Good Sam, started 25 years ago when a Utah trailerist sent a letter to *Trail-R-News* magazine (now called *Trailer Life*). The letter suggested that the magazine offer subscribers a decal for their rigs, something that would indicate their willingness to stop and help fellow RVers in distress. The idea caught on and mushroomed into the Good Sam Club.

Since few insurance companies were interested in covering RVs, it seemed only natural that the club should provide policies tailored to members' needs. Before long it became the major insurer of travel trailers and motorhomes.

Today there are over 750,000 members with 2200 chapters around the country. In addition to insurance with emergency road service, policy holders receive discounts at hundreds of campgrounds in the Good Sam Park program, a campground directory, a subscription to *Trailer Life* magazine, trip routing and even RV financing. (The insurance isn't mandatory for club membership.) Free services are: Mail forwarding (quarterly postage charges), credit card loss protection, lost key service, lost pet service, commission-free travelers checks and a monthly newsmagazine, the *Hi-Way Herald*.

Trailer Life, by the way, is a valuable publication for RV travelers, whether full-timers or weekenders. It is full of important news, features on how to repair your rig, interesting places to visit as well as general trends in the RV industry.

Escapees

There are several full-time RVer organizations, but the best-known and largest is the Escapees (SKP) with 12,000 members. Founded by Joe and Kay Peterson several years ago, the club has grown by leaps and bounds as more and more people discover the joys of full-timing.

The Escapees' national headquarters is at Rte #5, Box 310, Livingston, TX 77351, (409) 327-8873. The club publishes a monthly news magazine, which presents important news about rallies and get-togethers, new places to park, tips on equipment maintenance and hints for making life easier for people who make their homes on the road. Members report where they are and what they've been doing so friends can keep in touch. SKP members often remark, "We feel like we're part of a large, close-knit family."

Another important facility of the club is a mail forwarding and message service. An 800 telephone number takes phone messages from friends and relatives and the messages are retrieved by calling the same number. Mail is forwarded automatically. This solves the problem of keeping in touch with the world while gypsying.

Co-op RV Parks

One way of cutting expenses and owning your own lot is by joining a co-op park. A pioneer in this kind of development, the Escapees has a network of cooperatively-owned RV parks. The earlier ones were constructed as individual efforts on the part of a group of members, but lately the club has undertaken development on a more organized scale. Several of these parks, scattered from Florida to California, are member-owned and operated. A typical co-op park starts when a group of RV owners purchase a piece of land and begin recruiting other members who want to invest in an RV lot. By chipping in and doing the work themselves, they end up with a park with all the amenities, each member with a deeded piece of ground for a fraction of what they might spend with a commercial developer.

The problem of what to do with belongings is solved as co-op members build storage sheds on their lot. Sometimes the sheds become elaborate buildings with a living room and sleeping accommodations as well as storage. When the motor home or trailer is parked next to the structure, they have an instant house and guest room. We've seen some *two-story* affairs, with a large garage-opening in the middle to park the RV when the owners aren't traveling. The Escapee club rules mandate that co-ops devote a portion of each co-op park to free boondocking for Escapee members from other chapters who happen to be visiting.

The cost of a membership in a co-op varies with the location. For example: Paradise Park in Pahrump, Nevada (P.O. Box 819, Pahrump, NV 89041.), charges $4,250 for a full-hookup lot. Because the lots sold out shortly after the park opened, it's necessary to get on a waiting list for upcoming vacancies. In late 1991, the waiting time was about six months. Co-op members pay their own metered electricity plus a fair share of taxes, insurance, a manager's salary and other operational costs. Split 100 ways, the monthly costs are minimal. Co-ops keep costs down by renting spaces they've reserved for that purpose to travelers and temporary residents. Also, most members allow their lots to be rented when they aren't there; the manager handles this for them. All management decisions are made by vote of the members.

Homebase Advantages

There are other parks around the country where you can own your own RV lot. This is very different from buying a "time-share" membership which entitles you to limited-time camping privileges. In the ideal situation, you will obtain a deed to your own lot, you will own the property, you can leave your RV there as long as you wish, and finally, you will have a vote or say-so in the park management. In a situation like this, there are several advantages.

For one thing, you now have a home base, a place to receive mail and legal documents (and have it forwarded). Your home base is your place of legal residence, despite the fact that you could be traveling anywhere in the nation. Parks in Nevada, Texas, Washington and Florida offer additional advantages in that there are no state income taxes in these states. For most people trying to make it on a shoestring this isn't significant, but for folks with investment income, the savings could be welcome. Some states (California, for one) insist upon taxes on any money earned in that state, no matter where you live. Therefore, rental income on your huge Malibu home will be taxable, but the dividends on your million-dollar DuPont investments are free from state taxes.

Another advantage is having a place to leave your RV when not traveling. Instead of placing it in a $70 a month storage lot for half the year you simply leave it on your RV lot where it is watched over by neighbors and management. It's ready to use any time you're in the neighborhood, and it'll probably cost you far less than the storage lot.

RV Clubs for Singles

Of all the RV singles' clubs we've looked into, Loners on Wheels is our favorite. All the members we've interviewed are enthusiastic about the club and continually talk about what it has done for them. In Chapter Nine—dealing with singles and retire-ment—we will describe Loners on Wheels and Loners of America in more detail as well as several other singles clubs both RV and travel oriented.

Commercial Campground Memberships

Frankly, I've always felt skeptical about commercial membership clubs such as Thousand Trails, Coast to Coast and others, looking upon them with the same jaundiced eye as I do time-share condos. For $6,000 to $10,000 you receive "lifetime" rights to camp in a membership park for a limited number of days. Perhaps it's the postal come-ons that made me dubious. Getting a notice in the mail that I have won a fabulous prize always makes me suspicious, particularly when I learn that I have to sit through a sales pitch in order to receive my prize.

Like time-share vacation condo plans, these RV schemes involve large, long-term investments for a small, short-term usage. Why should someone invest this kind of money just for the privilege of parking in some inconvenient, out-of-the-way campground? For the average RV traveler, who makes a couple of two-week trips a year, it makes no sense at all. Better take that initiation fee and use it to stay where you want to instead of where you *have* to.

However, after talking to several full-time RV travelers, my opinion has shifted somewhat. Some dedicated full-timers have made a science of getting their money's worth from these campground memberships. They've learned how to take advantage of the $1 or $2 a night camping fees, by staying the allotted time—usually 14 days—then moving on to the next one. Some parks aren't strict about enforcing rules, and permit longer stays. For the full-timer, particularly those on a tight budget, detouring a few miles out of the way to take advantage of the $1 a night fees makes the membership worthwhile. "What do we care if the campground is 20 miles out of town?" asked one couple. "By staying a couple of weeks in each place, we cut our rent down to $30 a month! It doesn't take long to recoup our original investment at that rate."

Another caveat: please read any contract you sign *very carefully!* I recently read of a couple who bought a non-transferable membership for $1,000 from an RV resort. They thought it was a good deal, since it was near their home and they could use it often.

Then the resort lost its lease and had to close. They decided to drop their membership and eat the $1,000. Then they discovered that they had to put up an additional $1,000. It was in the contract.

Chapter Nine

Singles and Retirement

Perhaps you've noticed that the ads in most retirement publications picture typical retirees as a handsome couple, tenderly holding hands as they gaze lovingly upon their new retirement home (or Cadillac, yacht, whatever the ad is selling). The husband is attired in an Irish-tweed sportcoat and his distinguished platinum-toned hair sweeps back from an aristocratic forehead. (He's never bald as a pig's knuckle, now is he?) The wife's hairdo discretely displays a few silver highlights; if we didn't know she was retired we'd assume she was about 37 years old. This typical retired couple is successful, affluent and looking forward to a future of golf games, gourmet dinners and bridge parties as they entertain brilliantly in their fabulous new home.

You don't need someone to tell you that this picture is far from accurate. Besides the fact that few of us men can brag about our aristocratic-looking foreheads, most men look our ages and some are truly bald as pigs' knuckles. More importantly, a large percentage of retirement-aged people lack that loving other person to hold hands with. A huge number approach retirement alone. Furthermore, they find themselves far from affluent, with their minds on other matters than bridge parties and golf games.

What happens when your spouse dies unexpectedly? Just before your planned retirement date? All your plans get knocked into that famous cocked hat. What about the homemaker who spent her productive years raising a family, only to find herself divorced once the children are on their own. Where do you go from here?

Women and Retirement

For every 100 older men in the United States, there are 146 older women. This sex ratio increases with age to a high of 260 women for each 100 men for those 85 and older. Only 41 percent of these women are married, compared to 78 percent of the men. Furthermore, statistics show that more than half of America's women are on their own even *before* they reach retirement age— by the time they are 55 years old. Those divorced or widowed women who manage to find careers in the workplace often find their social lives revolving around work. But once single women leave the workplace, they find a void that needs to be filled by friends and family. Should a retired woman be short on either of these commodities, she faces a lonely future. Chances are, she will also be short on retirement funds as well. It's well known that women earn significantly less than men doing equal work, so they end up with lower Social Security payments, company pensions and savings accounts.

Women also have fewer options or activities that society considers "acceptable" and with which they feel comfortable. A man can be perfectly happy tent camping and fishing in the woods, wearing the same socks a week at a time. Most retired single women not only feel uncomfortable camping in a flimsy tent, but hate fishing in the first place. (Not to mention dirty socks.) A man thinks nothing of living just about anywhere, but most women feel apprehensive in all but the most secure situations.

According to the Social Security administration, the average "aged" couple draws $960 a month in Social Security benefits. (Presumably, "aged" means 65 or older, not "aged" as in well-aged brandy or well-aged champagne.) Yet single women in this age group average only $522 a month. Single people, both men and women, need different retirement strategies than married couples, but single women need even more than that. On $522 a month, they need miracles.

Single Transitions

One might think that transition into retirement would be easy for those who never married, or for those who have lived most of their adult lives as single persons. Why should retirement be a traumatic experience? After all, aren't they used to a single life? It might seem that the only thing to do now is adjust to a lifestyle that doesn't include working every day. Yet these people often find retirement especially lonely, particularly if their entire social life had centered around their jobs. At work, they had fellow employees to socialize with, friends to talk with and companions at lunch. When they stop working, suddenly all of that is gone. Also gone are regular paychecks, paid health care benefits and Christmas bonuses. It's a different world out there when you quit work.

For those fortunate enough to have built up a network of friends and acquaintances, leaving this umbrella probably doesn't make much sense. Even though you're living in an expensive area, you might be better off squeezing by and keeping your friends and your mode of living.

But if your friends do come mostly from your business or workplace world, and if you have few or no nearby family connections, you could find that you have little to lose by going someplace more economical, perhaps someplace with a nicer climate. You can then start building a new life, acquiring new friends and exploring new interests. If you're already living in a high-cost area, moving to someplace more economical might just be the ticket to a better life.

Trying It Out

In many economical retirement locations, a small furnished apartment can be found for $200 a month, including utilities. Of course, these apartments are small, but perfectly adequate for a single person trying to get by on a shoestring. For example, in the October 15, 1991 Grants Pass Courier (Oregon), a small studio apartment is listed for $185 (everything included) in the nearby town of Rogue River—a delightfully peaceful and pretty place for small-town living. Shopping is a four-minute walk from the door.

Once settled, you have the chance to see how you like the area, to start making friends and exploring a new lifestyle. As a new kid on the block, you'll find the best way to begin accumulating a new set of friends and acquaintances is through volunteer work. Go to the local senior citizens office and apply for work with the RSVP program, or whatever volunteer work force that's available.

Within days, you'll start building a new network, and before long will have more friends than you ever made through working every day. One of our correspondents, a retired man, told us that his strategy for making friends is through square-dancing. He says, "Just check with the clubs (Elks, Eagles, American Legion, etc.) as well as with the Chamber of Commerce."

Shared Housing

Chapter Two discusses the concept of shared housing, a particularly effective way for singles to find inexpensive living quarters. Renting a room in a house requires little commitment— while he or she investigates a new locality for retirement potential. The bonus is that they are not alone; there are housemates who act as a surrogate "family." House sharing is a particularly successful strategy for older women, when two, three or four pool their resources and enjoy a dignified, comfortable living arrangement. They don't want to live alone, yet they clearly cannot afford some of the high rents demanded nowadays. House sharing by singles is also a creative technique for living in an exclusive, high-rent area on a limited income. Remember, as an added bonus, the crime rates in expensive areas are generally low.

It can be very lonely cooking for one person in an empty house. A person who owns a home often finds that a compatible companion or two sharing house expenses makes perfectly good sense. (On the other hand, it could make equally good sense to sell the house, put the money into utility stocks and move in with someone else.)

House or apartment sharing opportunities are becoming more and more common by the day. A glance at any newspaper classified section usually turns up several ads seeking this kind of arrangement. Don't hesitate to place your own ad. This gives you the opportunity to interview several potential partners before making any decision. It goes without saying that compatibility is the highest ranking consideration in house sharing.

Retirement Communities

However, not everyone can be comfortable pulling up stakes and relocating as a stranger in a strange town, or living in someone else's home. A convenient, worry-free alternative for singles is the concept of a non-prepay retirement community, the kind where you simply rent by the month. This was discussed previously in Chapter Two. Again, I'll use an Oregon example. At a place called Oak Lane Retirement Community, one can rent a studio apartment for $660. This includes: three meals daily (served in the dining room), weekly housekeeping and linen service, 24-hour staffing, cable TV, social and recreational programs, scheduled transportation, off-street parking and all utilities except telephone. Thus, aside from medical insurance, clothing and gambling debts, your basic expenses are covered for just $660 a month! For many singles, Social Security will cover it. Of course, this facility is not exclusively for singles; for an additional $275 monthly, a couple receives the same services. A similar place in the same town charges $880 for slightly better accommodations, but this still seems like a shoestring to me.

There are several advantages in this type of living arrangement. Besides the fact that your living costs are absolutely predictable, you can explore the community to see whether this is desirable for your long-term retirement without having to make any serious commitment. The manager of this retirement facility points out that she encourages people to do a three-month trial before pulling up stakes in their home towns or doing anything drastic. "This is particularly important upon the death of a spouse. Too often the survivor isn't capable of making rational decisions for the time being. They feel isolated, lonely, with no stimulation, and trapped in an empty home. In a retirement community they are surrounded by friendly people; they take their meals in the dining room surrounded by other residents with whom to communicate. Since there are no long-term obligations, this is a relatively painless way to try out a new lifestyle as well as trying on a new community for size."

One caution: most of the residents will be older; there are no multigenerational retirement homes. For many, this is the last step before entering a rest home. But the price is right.

Don't think the above mentioned retirement community is a unique retirement situation. You'll find similar establishments all over the country. To locate them, simply open up the Yellow Pages to "Retirement," and some will surely be listed. To choose a retirement community in another city, visit your local library and ask for the section where they keep out-of-town phone books. Then choose the city or town where you might want to retire, check the listings for something that sounds nice, and do some shopping for price and quality. Don't expect to find a $660 monthly fee just anywhere, however. Monthly charges vary widely, depending upon the community and upon the quality of the facility.

Be careful about those places where you must "buy-in" to the facility or where you must sign a long-term lease. There is nothing wrong with these concepts; it's just that if you are looking around for low-cost retirement alternatives you probably aren't interested in putting up $50,000 non-refundable front money just to see whether you like your new retirement location. If you find you aren't happy, you would be in a far better position if all you were responsible for was a 30-day notice before you shove off. Also, don't expect to find these reasonable rents in a larger city or in an expensive area. Like everything else in an expensive location, the costs are likely to be extravagant, too.

When you find something you can afford, check it out. The best time to visit is for lunch or dinner, when you can sample the quality and variety of the food. How is the place decorated? How does the staff interact with residents? Are they professional, yet caring? It the place quiet or noisy? Do people seem friendly and do they socialize well? Don't hesitate to speak with residents and see how they like living there. Many retirement communities have furnished guest apartments set up for trial visits. At the least, arrange to stay a weekend or a week to get a feel of the place.

Clubs for Singles

During the research on this book, I came across a very interesting singles club, oriented around travel and putting singles in touch with each other. The national leader in the travel partner matching field is Travel Companion Exchange of Amityville, New York. This club thrives on matching folks for the specific purpose of travel. Travel Companion Exchange (TCE) brings together travelers of similar interests through a newsletter and computer match-up service. Members list their interests and describe the kind of travel companion they would like to find. Since single travelers pay a high penalty for traveling alone (a single booking is often as high as a double), it makes good sense to team up with someone to share experiences and expenses.

"This isn't a lonely hearts club or a dating service," says Jens Jurgen, the company president, "although it works well in that respect. We've had a lot of marriages. I remember one elderly lady who met and married a gentleman through the service. Then, a few years later I saw her name on the list again. Her husband had died during a trip on the Orient Express, so she signed up to find another one!"

He stated further that while men travelers more often prefer to travel with women, the women very often prefer other women companions—much less complicated that way. Sometimes a woman will seek a male companion on a strictly hands-off basis. They simply tour and dine together. Jurgen says, "I realize that opposite sex matches are not always platonic, but this does not trouble me. I'm catering to the needs I see in the mail, single people needing traveling companions." At any given time, the membership is about 2,000, with some dropping out as others join. The newsletter carries a wealth of travel information and tips that make it worthwhile just for its content.

For inexperienced, elderly or handicapped travelers, having a partner makes sense. Women traveling alone miss out a lot by being reluctant to visit some very interesting places. Having a companion—of either sex—gives them far greater freedom to explore and enjoy themselves. It goes without saying that you must be very careful when using this kind of service. You need to make it quite clear as to what the traveling relationship will be and what it will not be. TCE suggests that you meet and do some getting to know one another before setting out on adventures. One woman complained that her lady traveling companion "smoked like a chimney and wouldn't drive under 80 miles an hour." A few meetings beforehand might have avoided subsequent bad feelings. Though TCE is multigenerational in nature, there are plenty of retired members.

Singles and RV Retirement

It might seem that this section properly belongs in Chapter Seven, under the heading of RV Retirement. But because recreational vehicles make one of the more successful retirement strategies for singles, I'm confident it belongs here.

As part of the research for this book, I placed notices, letters-to-the-editor and advertisements in various magazines, pleading for information, tips and advice for folks who've retired on minimum budgets. To our surprise, the vast majority of the replies came from RV retirees, *single* RV retirees in particular. A letter in *Trailer Life* magazine and a questionnaire in the *Loners on Wheels* newsletter brought in a surprising number of heartwarming replies. Singles from all over the United States and Canada recounted their experiences and told others how to do the same thing. Their enthusiasm was catching. We decided to visit a Loners on Wheels gathering to see first-hand what it was all about.

So, one balmy January evening, my wife and I drove our motorhome off the pavement to make camp amongst thousands of trailers, campers and motorhomes in a California desert setting. This was a place few non-RV folks have ever heard of: Slab City. (For a complete description of Slab City, or the Slabs, see Chapter Seven.) During this visit, and subsequent ones, we interviewed many couples from all parts of the continent, from South Carolina to Alaska. But some of our most eye-opening interviews were with single retirees.

It was a pleasant, moonlit night, with a slight breeze blowing in from the nearby Salton Sea. We breathed deeply of sagebrush-perfumed air as we walked across the sandy desert to where the Loners on Wheels had their semi-permanent headquarters. Several official trailers were set up around a large cement slab, which served as a dance floor at night and as a shuffleboard court by day. Some men were building the evening's campfire while several women stood around discussing the day's events.

We explained that we were interviewing retirees and were interested in talking to single retirees. We had come to the right place; the campers were eager to talk to us. "Man or woman—life is a difficult experience to handle alone," remarked one single man who had just moved into retirement. "I've found the solution to my loneliness through RV travel and belonging to Loners on Wheels."

"Traveling with friends makes all the difference in the world," explained another LoW member. "I'd never have the courage to do it alone." With other club members in a caravan—always ready and willing to assist—RV traveling becomes relatively anxiety-free. Socializing over breakfast, cooking dinner together or singing around the evening campfire, there is no time to be bored or feel alone. Since most RV clubs have a philosophy of "Never let a stranger into camp without a hug," RV retirement becomes a heartwarming experience.

Loners on Wheels (or LoW) is just one of several RV clubs that cater exclusively to single travelers. Loners of America (LOA) is another of the major clubs of this type, actually a splinter from the original club. Almost all members are retired. All but a handful are over 60 years of age. Don't misunderstand, neither Loners on Wheels or Loners of America are senior citizen lonely hearts clubs or "swinging singles" groups. Far from it. These organizations fulfill a legitimate need in bringing people together for mutual support, assistance and companionship while traveling in RVs. If you join one of these groups looking for romance, you'll probably find it, but the club terminates your membership the moment you begin traveling with another person. That's not to say that many friendships haven't blossomed into marriages, but when this happens the members are declared to have "committed matrimony," given everyone's best wishes and then kicked out of the club. When they say "single" they mean just that! This policy avoids the stigma of a lonely hearts group and assures new members that they won't be pressured by romantic overtures unless they specifically invite them. With this implicit understanding, many women feel more in control, immune from unwanted sexual advances, and men who aren't interested in marriage aren't bothered by husband-hunting hussies.

A great many retired singles live in their rigs year-round, so this support group is vital. Others travel seasonally, either going south for the winter, or north for the summer, and staying in their homes the rest of the time. The idea of RV retirement for singles is an exciting concept, so I'd like to describe it in more detail.

Singles clubs for recreational vehicle owners, come in all sizes, shapes and philosophical approaches. Loners on Wheels is probably the largest and most successful. With several thousand members, the LoWs are adding members steadily as the word gets out. An information-packed newsletter keeps members in touch with each other and promotes social and travel events. Every issue lists local chapter news, tips on RV maintenance and news from individuals as they recount their adventures on the road. (The LoW's address is found in the Appendix with other organizations.)

One member, an 82-year-old lady named *Duchess Grubb*, said, "This Loners on Wheels club is a life-saving group that has literally gotten people out of wheelchairs; we have camp-outs and rallies going on every month somewhere and caravans going in all directions." Duchess lives in her RV half of each year, commuting from her Pacific Northwest home—where she spends summers—to Death Valley and the Salton Sea for the winter. When we called for a telephone interview, we had to wait half an hour for her to return our call because she was changing the oil in her motorhome in preparation for a club rally in Death Valley the following morning. Duchess is a fascinating example of how an active life, full of interesting adventures, can contribute to a longer, happier future. The following is her story:

"Perhaps I'm not the ordinary, run-of-the-mill RVer," Duchess explained, (a classic understatement if there ever was one). "I still do a lot of maintenance on my 20-year-old RV (with 200,000 miles on it), such as changing oil, lubricating, changing sparkplugs and filters—things like that. I belong to the LoW club, a pleasant and helpful group. We do mostly 'boondocking' on the desert at Slab City from October until April. Side trips to Mexico, Nevada and Arizona are always a pleasure.

"Since my retirement in 1975, I've been coast to coast, to Mexico, Alaska, Yellowknife (Northwest Territory) and Nova Scotia. I've driven from Washington to California so many times my dog knows all the rest areas along the way. We spend many nights in rest areas. At campouts there are members from all walks of life who are willing to do everything from taking your blood pressure to doing 'shade tree' mechanic work. One time I joined a caravan of 14 rigs (all women drivers) on a four-month tour of Alaska that cost around $2,000 each. We fished for salmon, panned for gold and filled our ice chests from the Portage Glacier.

"With the good Lord willing, and if the price of gasoline doesn't get too high, I hope to be good for another 100,000 miles and make many more friends in many far away places. By the way, we LoWs never say *goodbye*. We say S-Y-D-T-R, or *See You Down The Road!*"

Economics and Safety

Duchess Grubb reported that a budget of $800 a month more than adequately covers her lifestyle. She pointed out that many RVers live on nothing but Social Security and that membership in LoWs helps make this possible. For example, a recent campout-rally at a local fairgrounds (in Washington State) cost $50 for the full week, but that included complete hookups plus two meals a day. Most questionnaires filled out by singles club members described very economical living. One lady reported that she never needs electricity because her solar panels provide adequate energy. On an income of $11,000 a year, she maintains her motorhome, two cars, a paid-for home in a northern state. "I do everything I want to do with that money," she says, "and I get a property tax break because of my low income." She told of several friends who live full time in RVs on less than $600 a month. I would suspect that this isn't because they want to, but because of necessity. Still, it's comforting to know that a lifestyle like this is possible.

At most Loners on Wheels campouts, it turns out that about 60 percent of the campers were women. "How do you feel about safety out here in the desert," I asked one lady. She explained that she had been a bank teller before retirement, and added, "During the two years before I retired, I was held up at gunpoint five times! Now, ask me again how safe I feel here!"

Another lady, a widow, said, "If it weren't for this club and all of the wonderfully supportive friends in it, tonight I would be sitting alone watching television in a two-room apartment in downtown Seattle." She smiled at her friends and said, "I've never felt safer in my life."

One of the men, a retired accountant from Texas, said, "I belong to another RV club besides Loners on Wheels, but some-how I feel like a third wheel as a single man among all of those couples. Here, I feel like I belong."

Part of LoW's success is due to its very active officers and members. President Dick March was most helpful in gathering information from club members for this book. Jennie Studdard, a 68-year-old livewire, a member since 1987, defends the singles-only rule by saying, "Without it, there'd be a lot more jealousy and gossip."

Friendly Roamers

What happens to couples who fall in love, or who "commit matrimony" and have to leave the club? Often they join a club such as the Friendly Roamers. Membership is not restricted; either couples or singles are welcome. The philosophy here is that living arrangements aren't any of the club's business.

Now that may sound racy to some folks, particularly those of us who grew up in the days before the "pill" and when "living together" was scandalous. Here is what one couple, in their mid-70s, have to say about this:

"After dating a few months, we decided that we were truly in love with each other, and inasmuch as the years were flying by, we wanted to travel while we were still healthy. For one thing, we could not love each other any more if some priest, minister, rabbi or justice of the peace had performed a ceremony over us. And secondly, we were amazed to discover how the government discriminates against singles who marry. As singles we can jointly earn $50,000 before our Social Security becomes taxable, but if we marry, that figure drops to $32,000 ($16,000 each)."

Although this couple obviously aren't on a minimum income (not if they worry about a $32,000 income restriction) but the same kinds of discrimination applies to those on the bottom end of the scale. For example, in order to be eligible for SSI (Supplementary Security Income) a couple cannot earn over $630 a month, while two unmarried individuals can earn $854 between them and still draw SSI. The same principle applies to eligibility for food stamps and other government programs.

Friendly Roamers also publishes an excellent newsletter with up-to-date news about rallies, campouts and the whereabouts of members. One issue reported on an unusual RV trip by barge on the Mississippi. The trip was sponsored by Good Sam, but several Friendly Roamers joined, driving their rigs onto barges at New Orleans and following the river north to Natchez, Vicksburg and Baton Rouge.

What I Need (WIN)

Yet another philosophy of single travelers comes from a unique club known as *What I Need*. The club's founder (a woman from Nevada), emphasizes that the club is not slanted toward the retirement sector. "To date, all of our advertising has been directed to 'Working Age Singles'," she says. "This a camping and caravanning network of singles born during or since 1927."

The idea of WIN started when several younger, still-working club members, would meet at rallies or campouts of Loners on Wheels, Good Sam, Escapees and so forth. The majority of the others were retired, often with interests different from the working members. They didn't like being told who they could, or could not, have in their rigs. Typically, a conversation would come around to something like, "This is very nice, but WHAT I NEED is a place where I can meet more single RVers my age." Thus was formed the nucleus of WIN, a new organization that focused on a younger crowd and which forced no restrictions other than "respectability, respectfulness and responsibility" on its members.

Chapter Ten

Try Before You Buy

While doing research through the Midwest in late 1991, I stopped over in a small Ozark town, one that had been touted highly for retirement by a popular retirement guide. It was a pleasant looking place, with a friendly, small-town atmosphere and several good fishing lakes nearby.

Most of the folks I interviewed seemed to love the town. Property was inexpensive, the climate relatively mild and fishing was great. An added bonus was very low property taxes. Then I happened to meet a man who had retired there, and who hated it. He was in the process of moving away. I asked why.

"I was born and raised in Philadelphia," he explained, "and I've always been used to the city. I like to sleep late in the morning and stay up late at night. If I wanted a snack at midnight, there was always a restaurant open, or if I needed something from the grocery store, there was one nearby that was open 24 hours. But here, everything shuts down at eight o'clock in the evening. I tried to learn how to fish, but I've never been able to get the hang of it. I just don't fit in here."

When asked why he made the decision to move here in the first place, he replied, "Well, I read about this town in a retirement guide. According to the book, it was one of the top-rated retirement places in the country. I had just gone through a divorce, and decided this would be a great place to start over. It sounded pretty good on paper, but the book didn't say anything about this being a dry county. I was always used to having a couple of drinks after work and mingling with people. Here, in order to have a cocktail, I have to drive 35 miles to the next county, go to a package liquor store, bring it home and mix it myself. I hate to drink alone!"

It turns out that a few weeks previously he received an invitation to a party from one of the few friends he had been able to make. His first social event. The party was in the next town, about 15 miles away, and he felt comfortable having a few drinks since a "designated driver" volunteered to drive everyone home after the party. Unfortunately, on the way home, the designated driver was stopped at a police roadblock. Even though the designated driver hadn't had a drink, he was charged with "transporting drunks." The whole lot of them were tossed into jail and heavily fined. "I just don't fit in here," he repeated sadly.

The lesson here is: *Try it before you buy it.* This unhappy man could have saved himself a lot of time, money and effort had he done some investigation on his own and not blindly accepted someone else's statistical evaluation. A trip to this dream town and a few nights in a motel would have told him everything he needed to know.

What Retirement Guides Can't Tell You

Most feature articles and guide books that give ratings as to the best places to retire are aimed at an audience of fairly affluent people. The articles are usually written from the subjective view of someone who knows what he or she likes, and assumes everyone else has the same tastes. For example, some writers include items such as museums, operas and symphony orchestras in their criteria for a good place to live. Others look at the quality of medical care, counting the number of doctors in an area, the amount of money invested in hospitals, the number of CT scanners or MRIs available to physicians and give top ratings to cities where there is a medical school.

Frankly, I'd be more interested in how much I have to pay for an office visit, and how much an ordinary hospital room goes for in my town. If I can't afford to enter those fancy hospitals in the first place, the whole thing is academic. As for operas, symphonies and museums, I've asked friends who agree that these are necessary for quality living, yet when I asked how long it had been since they had visited any of these attractions, only one friend regularly attends concerts. Even though we like to visit our local museum when a new exhibit comes along, we wouldn't make that an important part of our retirement decision. We don't have to live in a city in order to attend a concert there or to use the space-age technology in the hospital.

The point is, by giving the same weight to concerts, museums and medical schools as for climate, reasonable housing costs and personal safety, the retirement picture becomes unrealistic for all but the affluent. What good is an opera house if you get mugged as you leave because the city is crime-ridden? What good are hospitals if they are so expensive that you go bankrupt before you can get across the lobby?

Some retirement guides are excellent sources for statistics and data on towns and cities that would be otherwise difficult to find. They can tell you a world of information that can help you decide whether a place is a viable candidate for retirement. But in the final analysis, you have to go there and see for yourself. You have to see what the retirement guide cannot tell you: will you love it, or will you hate it?

Use Your Vacations To Investigate

Ideally, you'll start your retirement search long before the day your company shakes hands and says goodbye. Instead of going to the same old place for vacations, try to visit someplace different each time. Look at each location as a possible place to live. Check out real estate prices. Look into apartment and house rentals. Are there the kinds of cultural events in town you will enjoy? A cultural event could be anything from light opera to hoisting a glass of beer at the corner tavern; the question is, will you be happy you moved there? Just looking closely, as if you truly intended to move there, will tell you a lot.

While you are there, be sure to drop in on the local senior citizens' center. Talk to the director and the members of the center to see just what kinds of services might be available should you decide to move there. A dynamic and full-service senior center could make a world of difference.

Another important consideration is public transportation. Over the past few years a large number of smaller towns in the United States have been stripped of inter-city bus service. The Greyhound Corporation was permitted to buy out their only competition, Trailways, and shut down all but the most profitable runs. If you choose to live in one of these towns, you ought to be aware that you will be totally dependent upon an automobile. Without a car, you'll be trapped. Your grandkids can't visit you by bus, and if the nearest airport is 100 miles away, you'll not be able to meet the incoming flight. They'll have no way to get from the airport to your home. Yes, you could take a taxi, but places that don't have bus services probably won't have a fleet of taxis at your disposal either. Besides, by the time you make a few 200-mile round trips by cab, you could have purchased your own cab. These conditions are something you probably wouldn't notice on a regular vacation. You can pick up on them if you pay attention.

Stop in at the local Chamber of Commerce office. A world of information can be found there. The level of enthusiasm and assistance of the Chamber staff clearly tells you something about the town's elected officials and businessmen's attitudes toward retirees. Most Chamber offices love to see retirees move into their towns; they recognize the advantages of retirement money coming into the economy and the valuable contributions retirees can make to the community. These offices will do just about anything to help you get settled and to convince you that living in their town is next to paradise. However, don't be surprised if the person behind the counter isn't the least bit interested in your idea of retiring in their town. My experience has been that a few Chamber of Commerce offices are staffed with minimum-wage employees who seem to resent folks coming in to ask questions and interfering with the novels they are reading. When this is the case, you can guess that the level of services and senior citizen participation in local affairs is somewhat inadequate.

Even if you are already retired, you need to do some traveling if you plan on moving somewhere else. Your travels needn't be expensive. Pick up some camping equipment at the next garage sale in your neighborhood—a tent, sleeping bags and a cooking stove. Just about anywhere you want to visit will have either state parks with campgrounds or commercial camps—places like KOA—where you can pitch a tent. Many RV parks have special spots for tent camping. Your local library will have at least one campground directory to help you locate one near your target town.

Newspaper Research

Between periods of travel, you can do your research at the local library or by mail. Almost all libraries have some out-of-town newspapers. The larger the library, the wider the variety. If you live in a small town where your library can't provide the newspapers you want (particularly those from another state or smaller towns some distance away), one way to obtain them is to write to the Chamber of Commerce in the place you are interested in and explain that you need a copy or two to make decisions about retiring there. You can also write to the newspaper office (look in the phone directory section of your library for the name of the paper). Some real estate brokers will gladly mail you copies of the local newspaper, because they know you will probably use their services when and if you decide to buy. We once had a real estate office send us a three-month subscription to the local paper to help us make up our mind.

A newspaper becomes a very valuable research tool. The most important section in an out-of-town paper is always the classifieds. Here you can check the prices of housing: home prices, rentals and mobile home parks. Compare them with your hometown newspaper and you begin to get a picture of relative costs. Look at the help-wanted ads and compare them to the *work*-wanted ads. You can see what the offered wages are, as well as the wages people are asking. This gives you an indication of what kind of earnings you can expect, should you look for part-time work, as well as what kind of competition you will have for jobs. Some classified pages have a special heading for "managers wanted," where you'll find positions managing apartment buildings, motels or trailer parks. Typically, these jobs offer free rent and perhaps a salary in return for a minimum amount of management work. Be careful, however, that you don't end up working full time just for rent!

If mobile home parks advertise spaces for rent, you know that the situation should be okay for buying a mobile home. If there are none available, you might find the condition described in Chapter Six where a mobile home will depreciate sharply. Compare the prices of used items such as furniture, appliances and automobiles against your paper's classifieds. If they are much higher, you can figure the cost of living is also higher.

Check the rest of the paper to get a flavor of what the town is like. See if the supermarket specials compare to those at home, particularly if there are national chains operating both places. Sometimes the identical specials will have differing prices from one locality to another; this can tell you something about prices. Look at the newspaper's editorial pages to observe management's political stance. It's very interesting how this can influence the thinking of a community. Look over the news stories to see if they are slanted heavily in the direction of politics instead of trying for a neutral position. Particularly revealing are campaigns for or against services and spending for senior citizen and low-income residents. If you are uncomfortable with the direction of the slant, this may be something you can investigate when you arrive in the town. It's impossible to tell for sure how local people think or vote by the way a newspaper presents its opinions, but often—when this paper is the only source of local news—these opinions are accepted as fact.

See how crime is reported in the local newspapers. This was discussed in Chapter Five. The way crime news is reported tells something about the crime climate in a town.

Newspapers should list senior citizen activities, cultural events like lectures and free concerts and often give news of community college classes open to seniors. Look for this menu of activities. See which ones are free, which ones cost money and which activities might interest you. A newspaper with a large section devoted to senior citizen news indicates a high level of interest in the well-being of retirees. Look for retiree political action groups. Wherever senior citizens band together to vote, the level of services and benefits rise in proportion to the voting strength.

Out-of-town telephone books are valuable adjuncts to newspapers for information. You can check for retirement homes, for apartment complexes that cater to seniors and get the address of the local housing authority office. If there is such a thing as subsidized housing available, they can tell you how to find it and how to apply. A telephone book's Yellow Pages can give you a picture of the business life in town. The number of banks, supermarkets, shopping centers and other commercial entities tells you something about the vitality of business. This is where you check for bus service and taxi companies. Look under the listing for "airlines" or "airports" to see if there is a local airport, and which airlines service it. A telephone book also gives an up-to-date listing for the Chamber of Commerce office and the senior citizen center. A letter to each of them could yield valuable information about the locality. A non-reply also tells you something.

After you've researched a community thoroughly by library research, you still need to visit in person.

Chapter Eleven

Foreign Retirement

In Chapter Seven we discussed RV retirement in Mexico during winter months. This can certainly be done on a shoestring. But spending a summer in Baja California would be only slightly less uncomfortable than spending a summer in a pizza oven. Therefore many tens of thousands of North Americans have discovered year-round on the Mexican mainland to be inexpensive, interesting and high-quality living. On the equivalent of Social Security, most find they can live in Mexico in a style far above what they could hope for at home.

A few years ago, Don Merwin and I co-authored a book, *CHOOSE MEXICO*, 1988, (Gateway Books, San Rafael, CA), which described how to retire in that country on a monthly expenditure of $400 a month. This fantastically low budget even allowed for servants and travel about the country! Conditions have changed over the years, just as they have in your home town, but the happy fact is, they haven't changed *that much* in Mexico.

Today, it takes approximately $600 a month to live in most parts of Mexico. Yes, you can also live on $600 a month in many parts of the United States, but the difference is: in Mexico $600 will provide a much higher standard of living. On $600, it's possible to rent a two-bedroom apartment, eat very well (including dining out at least once a week at a nice restaurant), and even have a cleaning lady in twice a week to take care of the house and do the laundry. As if that weren't enough, this budget covers medical insurance as well! Can you do all of that back home on twice that amount?

Sounds incredible? In 1991, my wife and I spent six weeks in Mexico doing research on the cost of living in the 1990s in order to update *CHOOSE MEXICO*. We traveled to a popular retirement area, rented an apartment for a month and kept scrupulous track of our expenditures. This time our budget came in at $601. The results were published in the October 1991 issue of the magazine *Transitions Abroad*. Here's how we did it:

We found a comfortable two-bedroom, two-bath apartment for $200 a month. Utilities (electricity and cooking gas) cost another $28. While our food budget in California runs over $250, in Mexico we ate just as well on $175. We spent $81 dining out and $44 on a catered cocktail party and dinner to repay some of the party invitations we accepted during this month. Laundry and a part-time cleaning lady accounted for an additional $30. Not counting our car—which we didn't drive during this month—our expenses came to $558. A major expense was buying the *Mexico City News*, 60 cents a day, for a $18 a month. A play and a guitar concert added another $25 to bring the total to $601, one dollar over budget.

Rent	$200
Food	175
Utilities	28
Dining out	81
Entertainment (cocktail party	44
Cleaning lady	30
Newspaper	18
Concert and play	25
Total	**$601**

Our full-coverage Mexican auto insurance for one car cost $240 a for the year ($20 a month). One can buy into the national health insurance program (free medicine, hospitals and doctors) for less than $20 a month, or get private insurance for $45 a month. A doctor's house call was only $13.33! Since we rarely visit doctors in the States, we didn't bother with the medical insurance. However, if we were staying year-round in Mexico, we probably would have opted for the $20 a month unlimited coverage. We easily could take that out of our entertainment expense. A typical dentist charges $100 for a porcelain crown and teeth cleaning costs $10.83 a visit.

Where North Americans Retire

Mexico is a large country, with an amazing variety of climates, landscapes and panoramas. From tropical Pacific beaches to high, snow-clad mountains, you can find any type of lifestyle imaginable in Mexico. However, unless you are fluent in Spanish, you probably will want to try your retirement in a place where there are many other North Americans to keep you company. That isn't because Mexicans aren't friendly; it's because you would soon become bored silly with no one to talk to, no one to communicate with.

So if you're looking for company, one place to go is to Guadalajara and its environs. More than 30,000 North Americans call this home. Between the city and the many small communities clustered around Lake Chapala, you'll find a wide assortment of English-speaking groups where you will be accepted as friends. Helping newcomers get their start in Mexico is part of the tradition.

Guadalajara is in the temperate highlands, a place the residents like to describe as a "place of perpetual spring." Others prefer the tropics, romantic places like Acapulco, Puerto Vallarta or Mazatlán. Even though these places have a deserved reputation as expensive, jet-set resorts, you'll discover that the North American retirees enjoy life on a different level: less expensive and less hectic. Although retiring in one of these communities on less than Social Security is entirely possible, it's best to figure on a little more.

Finally, there are many other locations in Mexico that make wonderful places to retire. From Baja to the Yucatán Peninsula, they are all described in the book *CHOOSE MEXICO*. Most libraries have a copy, so before you make any decisions, check it out.

Not for Indigents

Although it is absolutely possible to retire in a foreign country on a budget of $600 a month, I would feel uneasy recommending it to those who have no more than that amount of income to spend. There are too many unknown and unexpected expenses that inevitably will crop up and possibly cause problems. At least at home, there are "safety nets" of sorts to catch you should sudden disaster strike. There are county and state agencies who will make sure you are taken care of. In Mexico, you are on your own, or dependent upon the good graces of fellow North Americans; there is no welfare system in Mexico. Furthermore, if you are truly indigent, the Mexican government could take a very dim view of your being there. You are not permitted to work, and could be in trouble should you try.

Driving in Mexico

Most Mexican highways are adequately paved, but not designed for high-speed driving. Mexican drivers tend to drive slowly; they seem to believe that the slower they drive, the longer their vehicles will last. It's best to fall back into this mode, because we shouldn't be tearing up the highways anyway. The worst thing about Mexican highways is that they lack wide shoulders. Often there are no shoulders at all. This is fine for driving during the daytime, but *not* at night. *Never* drive at night! The roads are poorly lit and a collision with cattle (which are not properly fenced in) can be deadly for you as well as for them.

An even more important piece of driving advice is: never drive in Mexico without *Mexican* automobile insurance. Non-Mexican insurance is not valid. Fortunately, insurance is inexpensive if you buy from the right source. (Don't believe the guidebooks when they say all Mexican insurance costs the same.) Details on insurance and other essentials can be found in the book *RV TRAVEL IN MEXICO*, which I suggest you check out at your library. (If your librarian doesn't have it, scold her harshly and insist that she order it forthwith!) The book also lists over 400 RV parks in Mexico with prices and ratings.

Is Mexico Safe?

This frequently-asked question is frustrating to anyone who has traveled in Mexico to any extent. The misinformation and distorted pictures of Mexico that most folks carry in their minds are difficult to dispel without actually taking a trip into Mexico. The truth is, Mexican people are gentle, polite and extremely law-abiding. Oh, that our society could be as law-abiding as theirs!

Why? One reason is that the law there is very strict and tough on habitual criminals. Upon the third conviction, a criminal automatically receives a 20-year sentence—even though all three crimes were minor offenses. This discourages people from becoming criminals, as you can well imagine. People who go to Mexico often will tell you that they have no fear of walking the streets of an average Mexican town at any time, day or night.

I've heard many horror stories over the years about someone's brother-in-law's friend who had difficulties with the police when involved in a minor accident. Yet, during my 44 years of driving in Mexico (nearly 100,000 miles), I've never been unfairly hassled by police, and I've never personally met anyone who has! Where are all these brother-in-law's friends, anyway? I've interviewed many Americans who've been involved in accidents in Mexico, and they've had nothing but praise for their insurance companies and the local authorities.

In the January 1991 issue of *Loners on Wheels Newsletter*, a retired, single lady, driving her motorhome toward Cancun, Mexico, described an accident this way: "Two days into Mexico, like a turkey, I stopped for a feathered turkey sitting in the road. A big green truck loaded with oranges didn't stop. The trucker's insurance paid for my damages. It's strictly against the law in Mexico to hit anyone stopped on the road! The police and my insurance adjuster couldn't have been nicer. Two days later, the garage had miraculously patched up my RV, so my trip continued."

I'm sure bad things happen in Mexico, just as they can occur anywhere. Yet, I'm personally convinced that the incidents are fewer and farther between than here. One point that needs to be made, however, do not confuse the *mordida* (bite) that a police officer accepts with a bribe. If you speed, if you go through a stop light or stop sign, and a cop sees you, he will give you a ticket, just as will a cop in Toronto or Toledo. The difference is, you can pay the fine to the cop and avoid having him take your license plates and make you pay the ticket at the police station. This money is considered part of the cop's pay, and he is doing you a favor by taking it. However don't, under any circumstance, give a mordida if you are innocent. Doing so will only encourage inventing "traffic offenses." Believe me, most of the time a cop stops you in

Mexico, you've done something wrong. So offer him three or four bucks and let it go at that.

Central American Retirement

To a person who hates winter and who loves foreign living, places like Mexico, Guatemala and Costa Rica are extremely attractive. From the age of 17, when my family moved to Mexico, I've spent every winter possible enjoying its sunny warmth and charming tropical surroundings. Then I discovered Central America in 1977, with a three-month drive through Guatemala, Honduras, El Salvador, Nicaragua and finally Costa Rica. Thus began a love affair with this region that has continued through my early 1992 visit to complete research on my book about it.

Lamentably, all but one of the Central American countries have suffered hectic and tragic times recently. Things are getting much better, and tourists are once again visiting the region in growing numbers. Folks are beginning to think about retirement there. In fact there are 8,000 U.S. citizens retired in Central America, the majority in Costa Rica and most of the rest in Guatemala. The number of Canadian citizens is large, but the figures aren't readily available.

Costa Rica

Only Costa Rica avoided the civil problems that mired her sister republics in a quicksand of turmoil and tragedy. It alone remained a bastion of peaceful tranquility and a haven for American retirees. Costa Rica's devotion to democracy and peaceful cooperation with its neighbors helped it to retain its enviable position as a showcase of prosperity, respect for law and personal freedom. Partly because of this tradition of peace and democracy, partly because of the rugged, sometimes snow-capped mountains, Costa Rica is called "the Switzerland of the Americas."

As a foreign country, Costa Rica has one of the highest percentages of North Americans retirees living within its boundaries. There are several reasons for this besides the breathtaking beauty of the country. For one thing, the climate is one of the best in the world, with a choice of year-round spring climate in the Central Plateau or lush tropical beaches along the Pacific and

Caribbean coasts. Either coast is a short drive from the temperate central region.

Another attraction is a reasonable cost of living. Certainly inflation has hit Costa Rica over the past few years, but little more than in the United States, and clearly less than Mexico. Retirement on a shoestring is possible, since the average U.S. Social Security check is more than the average middle class Costa Rican earns. The government only requires an income of $600 a month to become a resident. However, as I cautioned about retirement in Mexico, or in any foreign country for that matter, it would be extremely unwise to try living there if you had no backup resources and if $600 was all you could count on.

For most North Americans, the biggest attraction for retirement in Costa Rica is Costa Rica's friendly citizens. This is an egalitarian country, where everyone considers himself equal to everybody else. The people are outgoing, happy, and they sincerely like North Americans because we are so much like them.

Tourists are restricted to 90 days visit at a time in Costa Rica, but that's long enough to get the flavor of living there to decide whether it would be an appropriate place for retirement. In San Jose, where most retirees live, or at least start out living, it is easy to rent one of the many apartments that are available by the week or month to get the essence of the country. Then, if they decide that they like it, they usually need to return to the States for documents and paper work. Like Mexico and Guatemala, the legal technicalities of retiring here are burdened with red tape, trips to various government ministries and rubber stamps marking everything in sight. However, those who manage to do all of this and still keep both oars in the water say it's all worth while.

Guatemala

Things are far better today, but for the past decade, Guatemala was plagued with problems that discouraged tourism and retirement. Despite this, at least 1,500 U.S. citizens and an undetermined number of Canadians have chosen retirement in Guatemala. Mostly they've settled around Antigua and Lake Atitlan. Of all the economical retirement styles described in this book, this has to be the bottom line of shoestring economics. An indication of this is that the government only requires a monthly income of $300 in order to obtain a *pensionado* or retiree resident visa.

One resident of Guatemala's Lake Atitlan was quoted in the Costa Rican *Tico Times* as saying, "A retired professor from the States doesn't enjoy a monumental pension, but here I can live like a majharaja, whereas in the States I'd be cashing in Green Stamps."

The local retirees put down the idea that there is anything dangerous about living there. One man told the *Tico Times*, "Being a Gringo, we're pretty much protected. It doesn't serve anyone's purpose to alienate the U.S." A lady retiree said, "Really, I feel safer here in Guatemala than I would in a neighborhood of Chicago or New York. Much safer."

I'm convinced this is true, however I must say that there are very *few* places in this world where I would *not* feel safer than in Chicago or New York! Beirut, Baghdad or Newark perhaps. Understand, this report on safety is second-hand, since my last drive into Guatemala was in 1983. However, I am scheduled to go there immediately after finishing this book to research Guatemala more thoroughly, and should come up with some answers of my own before long which will be included in the book *CHOOSE COSTA RICA* which will be published in 1992. (Tell your library to order it.)

Study-Retirement Program

One way of visiting Guatemala and trying it out is to attend one of the language schools there, studying Spanish. Not only is this a fascinating way of learning more about the country, but it is incredibly inexpensive. In Antigua, the location of many Spanish schools, room and board with a Guatemalan family can be arranged for $30 to $40 a week (that's $120 to $160 a month!) Schools provide one-on-one teaching for as little as $2 an hour.

One couple wanted to visit Guatemala and learn Spanish, but they decided to take their motorhome and use it for accommodations rather than stay with a Guatemalan family. Scott and Karen Bonis reported their experiences in *Escapees Newsletter* as follows:

"When we decided to go to a language school, we selected *Projecto Linguistico Francisco Marroquín* in Antigua. It is more expensive than others in the area, but it is where the U.S. Government sends its employees. You enroll by the week, so if it is not to your liking, you can change.

"The school is run by Pamela, a no-nonsense British expatriate, about 50 years old, who is a mother figure to nearly every gringo staying in town. She can solve most problems, from finding a place to stay to changing money (at a better rate than at the border). As a result, her office is a steady parade of people.

"We entered Guatemala with 30-day entry permits for ourselves and our vehicles. The standard procedure is to get extensions of the papers which requires a trip to Guatemala City. However, there are people who specialize in obtaining tourist papers for the beleaguered tourist.

"We parked at the Antigua Texaco station, a new, modern place with space for three small campers. We had water and electric and used the (cold) shower in their restroom.

"Our school consisted of four buildings scattered throughout the town, most of which were formerly homes of wealthy families. Students work one-on-one with a teacher, and one student-teacher pair occupies each room. The room contains one small table, two wooden chairs and a 40-watt light bulb. The windows, in general, do not have glass, but rather shutters and the requisite iron bars to prevent intruders.

"On top of each table is a pile of blank newsprint sheets, each about 24"x36", which are the 'blackboards' for the pair. If there are more students than rooms, tables are also scattered along the covered walkway surrounding the courtyard. Those students who return week after week can request specific teachers and/or rooms, which means the new students generally spend the first week in the courtyard.

"School occupied the majority of our waking hours. We attended seven hours a day, five days a week, with a two-hour break for lunch. We were so saturated with Spanish that studying at the break was impossible. At night we did a few chores, rushed home to dinner, and then studied.

"After two months we were able to appreciate 80 percent of the jokes told to us in Spanish by our teachers. We still made many grammatical errors, but all of the teachers were patient and humored us when we became depressed. We listened to the Mexican versions of soap operas, which tend to speak in slow, exaggerated phrases, and we could follow the plot. However, we still can't understand much of the news or street conversation because it is simply too fast for us.

"At first, the teachers spoke slowly and distinctly to us. By the time we left, they were speaking at nearly normal speed and we were really grasping their thoughts. It was truly amazing how much clearer all of the native people were speaking compared to how they used to speak when we arrived just two months before!

"We don't regret it for a minute. We learned an incredible amount of Spanish, however, it is only a beginning and we surely need to study further so, yes, we will go back."(With permission from *Escapees Newsletter,* September / October 1991.)

Peace Corps

For foreign retirement on a shoestring, here's the best option of all: join the Peace Corps! It isn't as crazy as it might seem at first glance. The Peace Corps actively seeks out older, retired citizens who have much to contribute. No other group in this country embodies the years of leadership, skills, experience and proven ability of our senior citizens. For the first time in their lives many senior citizens find themselves without commitments to a career or family, and they are finding fulfillment and excitement in the job of helping others. In addition, they're getting *paid* for it! They're having the time of their lives, and at the same time participating in programs that affect literacy, health, hunger and help promote world peace, friendship and sharing. Retired singles and couples have put their expertise to work in Africa, Asia, South America, Central America and the Pacific Islands.

Peace Corps volunteers receive living expenses and a monthly stipend to cover incidental needs, so there is no need for them to spend savings or other income. In addition, $175 per month is put aside and given to them at the end of the typical two-year assignment. This $4,200 per person comes in handy for making a transition back into life at home. The compensation you receive from the Peace Corps doesn't affect your Social Security earnings. Since all expenses are paid, many older Peace Corps volunteers bank their entire Social Security, pension and interest income during their two-year tour of duty.

Here is a terrific opportunity to make a contribution to peace, to utilize your life's experience helping others, and to have the *time of your life*. If you're married, odds are that your spouse also has some much-needed skill, so there's a chance that the two of you might go overseas as a team. For further information or an application, write to Peace Corps, Room P-301, Washington, D.C. 20526; or call, toll-free, 800-424-8580, ext. 93.

Chapter Twelve

Our Favorite Retirement Places

When someone suggested that we list of 50 of our favorite retirement locations, it sounded like an easy task. After all, my wife and I visited and inspected many, many parts of the country in the course of our research travels. However, when we sat down to compile our list, we discovered that we had to choose from a list of almost 300 nice places we had visited over the past seven years of retirement explorations.

We found it would be impossible to choose just 50 towns or cities. We would miss too many desirable retirement havens by restricting our list to specific towns or cities. Often, three or four places are clustered in a general area; areas like the Carolina coastlines, California's Gold Country or the Rio Grande Valley in Texas. Therefore, we organized our list into places—sometimes centered in a single town, sometimes scattered over an entire region.

Compiling this list of favorite retirement places made us even more aware of the subjective nature of what constitutes a "good" place to live. Between ourselves, my wife and I argued and discussed each location as to whether it should be included or ignored as a possible retirement haven. Many otherwise great places were eliminated because of economics. It wasn't easy; but we've never claimed that finding a retirement haven is an easy task.

Because we agree that these possibilities might suit our retirement needs, that doesn't necessarily mean they would be suitable for everyone. All of these places, plus the ones we eliminated from the list are described in greater detail in my book *WHERE TO RETIRE* (Gateway Books, 1991, see appendix).

ALABAMA

Dothan—Very popular with military retirees. Started with Panama Canal personnel settling here, and retirement boom continues. Real estate is reasonable, as can be expected in southern states. A bonus here is the cosmopolitan makeup of the local citizens; they come from all over the country, not just from the Deep South.

Fairhope—Small town on Mobile Bay with access to the Gulf of Mexico. It's attracted many retirees because of the gulf fishing and recreation opportunities, and its nearness to metropolitan areas. Several other small communities line the bay, most with retirement attractions similar to Fairhope.

ARKANSAS

Bull Shoals/Mountain Home—Small towns near great lake fishing. Some of the most reasonable property costs to be found anywhere near the Ozark lakes. Very friendly neighbors. These lakes extend into Missouri, where the towns of Branden and Camdenton also attract retirees.

Eureka Springs—A delightful Ozark mountain town, like a page from the past, with hot springs and Victorian homes, many at bargain prices. The relatively mild climate makes this an ideal retirement area. Not too far away is Fayetteville, a college town with a surprisingly rich cultural atmosphere, near fishing, hunting and Ozark beauty. Lots of city services yet a short distance from hunting, fishing and all that goes with outdoor sports.

Hot Springs—A small city in a picturesque canyon, with its famous hot springs as the center. Once very popular as a resort, Hot Springs real estate is now a bargain for those looking for a pleasant retirement location. Other Arkansas towns on the fringes of the Ozark, places like Heber Springs and Fairhope also draw retirees.

ARIZONA

Ajo/Bisbee—Two examples of western mining towns that draw bargain-hunting retirees when large mining corporations suddenly close down operations, sending the towns into economic tailspins. This forces property values down to once in a lifetime asking prices.

Lake Havasu City/Parker/Bullhead City—Wonderful desert retirement towns on the banks of the Colorado River. Hot in the summer, but pleasantly warm and dry in the winter. Laughlin,

Nevada is also included in this complex, for gambling and casino fun for those who dare risk their shoestrings on a green felt table.

CALIFORNIA

Burney/Fall River Mills—Tucked away in California's northern mountains, these are examples two undiscovered gems of beauty and retirement bargains. Outdoor recreation is good year-round and property is inexpensive.

Chico—The state university takes Chico out of the realm of an ordinary California small city, and brings retirees a myriad of cultural events as well as inexpensive living.

Dunsmuir—Clinging to the banks of the Sacramento River as it wends its way through a narrow canyon, Dunsmuir offers an outdoor wonderland and rustic old homes at bargain prices. A recent insecticide spill in the river has depressed tourism and housing prices. However, it is just a matter of time until it recovers.

Eureka/Fort Bragg/Mendocino—Along California's rugged northern coasts are a string of pleasant towns which offer quality retirement with a superb climate for those who hate hot and cold weather.

Gold Rush Country—Angels Camp, Fiddletown, Calaveras and a host of other famous boomtowns of the 49er days attract tourists and retirees alike. These picturesque locations not only offer an historical ambiance, but reasonable housing and mild winters.

Yucaipa—An example of high-desert living, not too far from Palm Springs and Desert Hot Springs. With an altitude higher than either of these places, Yucaipa enjoys cooler summers. Many inexpensive mobile home parks are around here.

COLORADO

Denver—Hit very hard by a crash in the real estate market, for a while Denver offered some of the best buys in the country. Although it's recovering somewhat, there are still bargains to be discovered.

Grand Junction/Battlement Mesa—Another place where the economy suffered because of the oil shale boom and bust, the Grand Junction area became famous for low-cost real estate. Local businesses actively campaign for retirees to settle there.

FLORIDA

Daytona Beach/St. Augustine—Lots of low-cost housing and reasonable apartments in this area. Good beaches and senior citizen services available.

Fort Walton Beach/Panama City/Pensacola—This Gulf of Mexico stretch of beach towns offer good fishing and beach recreation and fairly reasonable living costs, particularly in off-season.

Ocala/Orlando—Inland Florida is quite rural once away from the metropolitan districts. Farms and acreage are priced less than one might expect.

Sarasota/St. Petersburg-Tampa/Ft. Meyers—West Coast Florida can be considerably less expensive than the "Gold Coast" glitter around Miami. Too many apartment buildings mean lower rentals.

GEORGIA

Habersham County—An area of picturesque, low mountains, within an hour's drive of Atlanta. A place to investigate for those who like small town, rural living

KENTUCKY

Bowling Green—A living stereotype of Kentucky, complete with bluegrass, thoroughbreds and friendly neighbors.

Murray—Pleasant and economical real estate, typical of small cities along the Kentucky-Tennessee border. Recent publicity brought influx of outsiders into Murray, so prices are no longer dirt cheap.

LOUISIANA

Baton Rouge—A university town, with intellectual atmosphere and retirees from all parts of the country. Quality real estate for rock bottom prices here.

Houma—Typical Louisiana small town living. May not be appropriate for Northerners who aren't used to nuances of rural south. Leesville, to the north is another small town, but with large military influence and retirees from other parts of the country.

MISSOURI

Branson/Lake Tanneycomo/Lake of the Ozarks—Network of lakes in Ozark make for recreation-filled retirement. Housing costs are competitive and good highways take residents to St. Louis for heavy-duty shopping. The Lake of the Ozarks area is the most commercial, with good shopping, restaurants and entertainment. The other areas are more rural and isolated.

MISSISSIPPI

Gulfport-Biloxi—A string of pleasant retirement communities— Bay St. Louis, Long Beach and Pass Christian—attract northerners and military retirees because of pleasant ambiance and low housing costs.

NORTH CAROLINA

Asheville—Population center of the area, with university atmosphere as well as picturesque, Appalachian foothill location. Nearby Hendersonville and Brevard have received high ratings for retirement possibilities.
Blowing Rock/Boone/Newland—Gorgeous settings in the Great Smoky Mountains draw many retirees in search of milder summers and picturesque winters. Living costs range from very low to very high.

NEW MEXICO

Albuquerque—Dry weather climate and a university-assisted cultural climate combined with reasonable cost of living make Albuquerque a favorite.
Carlsbad—A small city that is actively encouraging retirees to relocate. Local Chamber of Commerce very helpful. Las Cruces and Truth or Consequences are also worth considering, with Las Cruces closer to El Paso, Truth or Consequences closer to Albuquerque.

NEVADA

Las Vegas and Reno—Local casinos make it a point to hire senior citizens as part-time workers. Although cost of living is higher, the employment opportunities and gambling excitement make it worthwhile for some.

OKLAHOMA

Grand Lake o' the Cherokees and Tenkiller Lake—Part of a large network of lakes on the fringes of the Ozark Mountains. Some of the cheapest real estate in the nation is found here. Some places are very isolated, however.

OREGON

Ashland, Medford, Grants Pass, Eugene—Inland Oregon valley cities, with quality living, academic atmosphere and low housing costs make these towns popular with California retirees. Mild winters, with very little snow and year-round greenness.

Bend/Klamath Falls—High-mountain locations, with pleasant summers, but lots of cold weather and snow to cancel things out in the winter. Hunting and fishing excellent.

Oregon Coast—All along the coast, interspersed between beaches and cliffs are places such as Brookings, Coos Bay, Florence, Gold Beach and Port Orford. Here the temperature is probably the most even in the country with no freezing days and no hot days. Real estate is bargain-priced.

SOUTH CAROLINA

Aiken—A lovely, Deep South city, with a mixture of northern and southern retirees taking advantage of retirement opportunities. At one time, this was one of the best buyer and renter real estate markets in the country. Still not bad.

Charleston—Perhaps the loveliest of the antebellum southern cities, Charleston offers an elegant mode of living not found elsewhere. Much housing is expensive, but there are some bargains to be found if one looks.

Myrtle Beach—A summer beach resort that has lots of retirees from the North who enjoy the seashore and mild winters. Many reasonable prices and rentals to the south of here.

TENNESSEE

Clarksville—Because of the large military base here, this has become a popular retirement place for servicemen from all parts of the country. An exceptionally friendly population and reasonable costs are the pluses.

Crossville—In a rolling countryside, wooded and agricultural, Crossville is typical of many Tennessee-Kentucky mid-sized towns. Nearby Fairfield Glen attracts retirees from Michigan, Ohio and Indiana.

Dover—A small Tennessee town with very inexpensive costs, which is becoming popular because of its proximity to the Land Between the Lakes and its outdoor recreational opportunities.

TEXAS

Austin and San Antonio—Two of the bargain places for real estate and apartment rentals. Overbuilding has caused prices to remain stable or to drop in a market of ever-increasing costs. Mild climates and cultural activities add to the attraction.

Corpus Christi and Galveston—Texas Gulf coast retirement attractions. Great water sports, mild climate and endless beaches combine with a low cost of living to make these worth investigation.

El Paso and Laredo—Border towns with easy access to Mexico for shopping and recreation, these rank very low in cost-of-living. Because of labor competition across the border, decent-paying part-time jobs are scarce if not impossible to find.

Rio Grande Valley: Harlingen/McAllen—The choice of countless part-time retirees, this area fills up every winter, only to become all but vacant in the summer. For those who can stand summer heat, they'll find rock-bottom prices here.

UTAH

Cedar City and St. George—The most popular places in the state for retirement. Real estate has been depressed for some time, causing distress sales and rental bargains. Both are close to skiing and outdoor recreation, but St. George is by far the more charming location.

WASHINGTON

Goldendale—In the southern part of the state with a beautiful setting, Goldendale is actively soliciting retirees. This is just one of many smaller towns who are rolling out the welcome mat for retirees. Housing prices are sometimes incredibly low, and rents seem like a gift.

Aberdeen—An example of a place in economic doldrums, Aberdeen has been hit by the double whammy of lumber and fishing slumps. Real estate prices and rentals were among the lowest we've ever seen. Like all Northwest locations near the ocean, Aberdeen's weather is perfect for those who hate freezing weather and hot summers. But it's terrible for those who love hot sunshine.

Appendix

RECOMMENDED READING

AMERICAN HIKING SOCIETY. *Helping Out in the Outdoors.* Yearly publication.

Over 100 pages of volunteer opportunities throughout the country at city, county, state and national parks. Most have free hook-ups for RVs and some have housing for non-RV folks. Some jobs pay a small salary. Order from American Hiking Society, 1015 31st Street, N.W., Washington, DC 20007

COMMUNITIES PUBLICATIONS COOPERATIVE. *Intentional Communities,* A Guide to Cooperative Living. Stelle, Ill., 1991

Complete listing of communities of alternative housing experiments.

FROMER, ARTHUR. *New World of Travel.* Prentice Hall, New York, 1990.

A must-have book for travelers. Covers alternative ways to travel, interesting vacations and long-term travel, house-swapping at home and abroad, volunteer opportunities and much more.

HOWELLS and MERWIN. *Choose Mexico.* Gateway Books, San Rafael, Calif., 1988

How to retire in Mexico and have a gracious, interesting life for very little money. Descriptions of the country and tips on where to retire. (New edition due in Spring 1992)

HOWELLS, JOHN. *Choose Latin America.* Gateway Books, San Rafael, Calif., 1986

Long term travel and retirement in Latin America. Covers Costa Rica, Mexico, Argentina, Brazil and most other countries in Central and South America. (Book is out of print, but should be in local libraries.)

HOWELLS, JOHN. *Where to Retire.* Gateway Books, San Rafael, Calif., 1991

A handbook of retirement, with detailed descriptions of over 100 retirement locations. Weather and crime statistics as well as unusual retirement opportunities.

HOWELLS, JOHN. *RV Travel in Mexico.* Gateway Books, San Rafael, Calif., 1989

> The how-to-do-it book on RV travel in Mexico. Tips on traveling in comfort and safety, where to go, how to deal with local people, plus complete listings of over 400 parks in Mexico.

HOWELLS, and MAGEE. *Choose Spain.* Gateway Books, San Rafael, Calif., 1990

> A comprehensive guide to retirement living in Spain and Portugal.

McMILLON, BILL. *Volunteer Vacations.* Chicago Review Press, 1989.

> A directory of short-term adventures that will benefit you, and others.

PETERSON, KAY. *Home is Where You Park It.* RoVers Publications, Livingston, Texas, 1989

> A how-to-do-it manual on full-time RVing, with tips on how to get started and to adjust to a new lifestyle.

PETERSON, JOE and KAY. *Encyclopedia for RVers.* RoVers Publications, Livingston, Texas, 1989

> Full of information on all aspects of RV travel as well as a complete list of services, organizations, publications and essential addresses for RV travelers.

PORCINO, JANE. *Living Longer, Living Better. Adventures in Community Housing for those in the Second Half of Life.* Continuum Publishing Co., New York. 1990

> Strategies for midlife and older people who value their independence but don't want to live alone.

Volunteer! Council on International Educational Exchange, 1990.

> A comprehensive guide to voluntary service in the U.S. and abroad, 1990-91 edition. A listing of short term to long term projects.

SYMONS, ALLENE and PARKER, JANE, *Adventures Abroad.* Gateway Books, San Rafael, Calif., 1991

> First-hand descriptions of retirement living in 12 countries. Information on housing, medical care, laws, finances and security.

Periodicals

Escapees Newsletter—Route 5, Box 310, Livingston, TX 77351. (409) 327-8873

Bimonthly publication of Escapee, Inc. (SKP), an organization that specializes in full-time RV travelers. Full of information for any RV owner.

Tico Times—Tico Times, Apdo 4632, San Jose, Costa Rica.
Costa Rican daily newspaper in English, printed in San José Costa Rica. A must for anyone planning on visiting this country. Yearly subscription is $20.

Workamper News—201 Hiram Road, Heber Springs, AR 72543. (800) 446-5627 (subscriptions only)
Excellent publication listing temporary and long-term jobs for RV travelers. Free employment and situation-wanted ads. A 24 page publication every other month. By subscription only, $18 a year.

Medicare Publications

The following are available from the Federal Consumer Information Center, Dept. 59, Pueblo CO 81009, or the Office of Public Affairs, Health Care Financing Administration, 200 Independence Ave. SW, Washington, DC 20201.
1991 Medicare Handbook (HCFA 10050).
Guide to Health Insurance for People with Medicare (HCFA 02110)
Hospice Benefits Under Medicare (HCFA 02154)
Medicare and Coordinated Care Plans (HCFA 02143)
Getting a Second Opinion (HCFA 02114)

INFORMATION SOURCES

Regional Offices, National Park Service

Contact these offices for information on specific volunteer programs.

Oregon
P.O. Box 2965, 729 NE Oregon St., Portland, OR. (503) 234-3361, Ext 4024

Pacific Northwest Region
Pike Bldg., 1424 Fourth Ave., Seattle, WA 98101. (206) 442-5542

Rocky Mountain Region
655 Parfet St., Box 25287, Denver, CO 80225. (303) 234-3095

Southwest Region
Old Santa Fe Trail, Box 728, Santa Fe, NM 87501. (505) 988-6340

Utah Region
P.O. Box 11505, Salt Lake City, UT 84111. (801) 524-5311

Western Region
450 Golden Gate Ave., San Francisco, CA 94012. (415) 556-4122

Headquarter Offices, State Parks

Contact these offices for information on specific volunteer programs.

Alaska Division of Parks
323 E. Fourth Ave., Anchorage, AK 99501. (907) 274-4676

Arizona Park Board
1688 W. Adams, Phoenix, AZ 85007. (602) 271-4174

California Dept of Parks & Rec.
P.O. Box 2390, Sacramento, CA 95811. (916) 445-6477

Idaho Dept. of Parks
Capitol Building, Boise, ID 83720. (208) 384-2154

Nevada State Parks System
210 S. Fall St. #221, Carson City, NV 89701. (702) 885-4370

Oregon States Park Branch
300 State Highway Bldg., Salem, OR 97301.

Utah Div. of Parks & Rec.
1596 W. North Temple, Salt Lake City, UT 84116. (801) 328-6011

Washington Parks & Rec.
P.O. Box 1128, Olympia, WA 98504. (206) 753-5755

RV Travel Clubs

There are at least 40 nationally-known RV clubs catering to individual interests of members. Many are sponsored by manufacturers of motorhomes or travel trailers as public relations efforts. While manufacturers sponsor the clubs, they rely heavily on the volunteer spirit among club members to keep the organizations flying. Below is a list of the ones we have heard about. We do *not* necessarily endorse clubs; some we know are worthwhile, while others we know nothing about.

Alpenlite Travel Club
P.O. Box 9152, Yakima, Wash. 98909

American Clipper Owners Club
514 Washington Street, Marina Del Rey, California 90292

Avion Travelcade Club
P.O. Box 236, De Bary, FL 32713

Baby Boomers
P.O. Box 23, Stoneham, CO 80754

Barth Ranger Club
P.O. Box 768, Milford, IN 46542

Beaver Ambassador Club
20545 Murray Road, Bend, OR 97701

Canadian Family Camping Federation
P.O. Box 397, Rexdale, Ontario, Canada M9W 1R3

Carriage Travel Club
P.O. Box 246, Millersburg, IN 46543

Champion Fleet Owners Association
5573 E. North St., Dryden, MI 48428

Cortez National Motorhome Club
11022 E. Daines Dr., Temple City, CA 91780

El Dorado Caravan
P.O. Box 266, Minneapolis KN 67467

Elkhart Traveler Club
2211 W. Wilden Ave., Goshen, IN 46526

Escapees, Inc. (SKP)
Route 5 Box 310, Livingston, TX 77351

Family Motor Coach Assoc.
P.O. Box 44209, Cincinnati, OH 45244

Fan Trailer Club
Route 7, Box 348, New Castle, Penn. 16102

Fireball Caravaner
12087 Lopez Canyon Rd., San Fernando, CA 91342

First Xplorer
3950 Burnsline Rd., Brown City, MI 48416

Foremost Motorcade Club
1221 N.W. Stallings Dr., Nacogdoches, TX 75961

Friendly Roamers
P.O. Box 3393, North Shore, CA 92254

Good Sam RV Owners Club
29901 Agoura Rd. Agoura, CA 91301

Happy Wheelers International
P.O. Box 503, Mishawaka, IN 46544

Handicapped Travel Club
667 J Ave., Coronado, CA 92118

Holiday Rambler RV Club
400 Indiana Ave., Wakarusa, IN 46573

International Country Club
P.O. Box 207, Junction City, OR 97448

International Coachmen Caravan Club
P.O. Box 30, Middlebury, IN 46540

International Family Recreation Assoc.
P.O. Box 6279, Pensacola, FL 32503

International Skamper Camper Club
P.O. Box 338, Bristol, IN 46507

Jayco Safari
P.O. Box 1012, Mishawaka, IN 46544

Lazy Daze Caravan Club
4303 E. Mission Blvd., Pomona, CA 91766

Loners on Wheels (See Singles Clubs)

Loners of America (See Singles Clubs)

Mobile Missionary Assistance Prog.
1736 North Sierra Bonita Ave., Pasadena, CA 91104

National Association of Trailer Owners
Box 1418, 2105 Tuttle, Sarasota, FL 33578

National Campers and Hikers Assoc.
4804 Transit Rd. Bldg. 2, Depew, NY 14043

National RV Owners Club
P.O. Box 17148, Pensacola FL 32522

North American Family Campers Assoc.
P.O. Box 730, Dracut, MA 01826

Rockwood Travel Club
P.O. Box 991, Mishawaka, IN 46544

RV Birdwatchers Club
409 Washington Ave., Loogootee, IN 47553

Serro Scotty Club
450 Arona Rd., Irwin, PA 15642

Silver Streak Trailer Club
226 Grand Avenue #207, Long Beach, CA 90803

Special Military Active Retired Travel Club
P.O. Box 730, Fallbrook, Ca 92028

Sportscoach Owners Intl.
3550 Foothill Blvd., Glendale, CA 91214

Starcraft Campers Club
P.O. Box 913, Mishawaka, IN 46544

Streamline Royal Rovers
808 Clebud Dr., Euless, TX 76040

Travel America Club
11 North Skokie Highway, Lake Bluff, IL 60044

Wally Byam Caravan Club
803 E. Pike St., Jackson Center, OH 45334

Wings of Shasta Travel Club
P.O. Box 912, Middlebury, IN 46540

Winnebago Itasca-Travelers
P.O. Box 268, Forest City, IA 50435

Clubs for Single RV Travelers

(From The Revised Encyclopedia for RVers, Joe and Kay Peterson)

Fifty Upward Network (FUN)
P.O. Box 4714, Cleveland, OH 44126
For middle-aged *women* who are divorced or widowed. Provides support and encorages self-validation through disucssion groups, meetings and seminars. Bimonthly newsletter.

Loners on Wheels
P.O. Box 1355 Lester Street, Popular Bluff, MO 63901
For single men and women who travel in their own RVs. Single only. Monthly newsletter, Rallies and informal caravaning. Dues $24.

Loners of America
191 Villa Del Rio Blvd., Boca Ratan, FL 33432
Member-owned and operated singles RV club. We understand this is an offshoot from the Loaners on Wheels. Dues $20.

Partners in Travel
P.O. Box 491145, Los Angeles, CA 90049
For those seeking travel companions. Bimonthly newsletter contains lots of travel information. $40/year or $5 sample copy.

Retired Singles
P.O. Box 642, Yucaipa, CA 92399
Computer matching service to unite singles who like camping and travel. Monthly letter. Fee: $50 for *six months.*

Solo Center
6514 35th Avenue Northeast, Seattle WA 98115
Services: resource, information and referral program for adults and families in transition by reason of divorce, separation, or death. Social and emotional support system. Phone: (206) 522-7656.

Travel Companion Exchange
Box 833, Amityville, NY 11701
Fee ranges from $5 to $11 a month. Write for information.

Travel Partners Club
Box 2368, Crystal River, FL 32629
Most members are widowed. Membership is $40 a year which includes a bimonthly newsletter.

What I Need (WIN)
P.O. Box 2010, Sparks, NV 89432-2010
A social club for single RV owners born after 1926. First year $25, then $20/year thereafter. Newsletter and rallies.

Naturist RV Resorts

To visit these clothing-optional resorts, please call ahead and expect a thorough screening designed to keep out thrill-seekers and deviants. All provide both tent and RV camping, and most also have cabins or rooms available. Further information on other clubs can be obtained by writing: American Sunbathing Association, 1703 N. Main St., Kissimmee, FL 32743-3386.

Index

instant housing, 87
parks, 77
pitfalls, 80-84
rock-bottom living, 84, 85

N
national parks
   free RV parking, 119, 120
   jobs, 119, 120
newspaper
   research, 146, 147,
   resources, 53-55

O
owning versus renting, 26-29

P
part-time instructing, 64, 64
part-time jobs, 57-59
Peace Corps, 158, 159
poverty line, 19
   and women, 20

Q
Qualified Medicare Beneficiary
   Program, 45, 46

R
real estate bargains, 33
retirement
   communities, 132-134
   guides, 143, 144
   strategies, 21-39
RV
   clubs, 122
   getting started, 115
   parks, 91
   RVs and Retirement, 89-107

S
safest cities and towns, 75, 76
sales work, 60
saving on utilities, 67-69
senior boomers, 17-19
senior citizens services, 47-52
singles
   clubs, 134, 135
   retirement, 129-141
   RV clubs, 126
   shared housing, 132
   transition, 130, 131
snowbirds, 71
Social Security, 19-21, 57-59
   disability, 46
SSI, 46, 47
starting your own business, 61
study-retirement program, 156

T
try before you buy, 142-148

U
utilities, 67-69
underground economy, 63

V
vacations, using to investigate,
   144, 145
volunteering, 52, 53, 57, 119

W
weather
   and your automobile, 69, 70,
   cool summers, 93, 94
   utility use, 67-79
Whole Work Catalog, 62
winter retirement, 90
wintering in Mexico., 103
women and retirement, 130
working and retirement, 56-65

About the Author

John Howells is the author of seven books on retirement strategies and locations in the United States and abroad. His writing on this subject has been praised by reviewers in many of the country's leading newspapers and magazines. He and his wife, Sherry, traveled back and forth across the United States by automobile, motorhome and airplane to conduct the research that resulted in this book. They talked with innumerable retirees and visited senior citizens centers, chambers of commerce, newspaper offices—anywhere they could get current information on retirement lifestyles.

At the time of *Retirement on a Shoestring*'s publication, John was in Central America, completing the research for a book on retirement in Costa Rica and Guatamala.

Our books are available in most bookstores. However, if you have difficulty finding them, we will be happy to ship them to you directly. Mail us this coupon with your check or money order and they'll be on their way to you within days.

Retirement in the U.S.

Strategies for comfortable retirement on Social Security
RETIREMENT ON A SHOESTRING $ 6.95 _____

Detailed information on America's 100 Best Places to Retire
WHERE TO RETIRE   12.95 _____

Foreign Retirement

Exploring the Travel/Retirement Option
ADVENTURES ABROAD   12.95 _____

Retire on $600 a Month
CHOOSE MEXICO: (Available in May 1992)   10.95 _____

Leisurely Vacations or Affordable Retirement
CHOOSE SPAIN   11.95 _____

Travel

The Complete How-to-do-it Book
RV TRAVEL IN MEXICO   9.95 _____

A Guide for the Mature Traveler
GET UP AND GO: 10.95 _____

Subtotal: _____

Add $1.75 for postage and handling for the first book, .50 for each additional one.
(Canadian orders: $ .75 additional postage)   _____

California residents add sales tax _____

Total Enclosed: _____

Credit Card Orders Only • Call our FREE number: 1-800-669-0773

Name_____

Address_____

City/State/Zip_____

Books should reach you in two or three weeks. If you are dissatisfied for any reason, the price of the books will be refunded in full.

Mail to: Gateway Books • 13 Bedford Cove • San Rafael, CA